The
ESSENTIAL
Gardening
Made Easy

Perennials
for SUN

INTERNATIONAL MASTERS PUBLISHERS, INC.

Printed and Manufactured in China.

ISBN: 1-892207-14-1

US P 0701 11 001

CONTENTS

WELCOME

The ESSENTIAL
Gardening Made Easy
Perennials for Sun

THE FIRST RULE OF gardening is that there are no rules—you are restricted only by your imagination. Gardening is about not only discovering what is right for your climate, but also about what you find aesthetically pleasing. If you've always dreamed of transforming your property into a lush, vibrant garden retreat but didn't know how or where to begin, you'll find the answers in *The Essential Gardening Made Easy*.

This series gives you the tools you need to create the garden of your dreams. To guide your creativity, the volumes are conveniently divided into three comprehensive sections: "Garden Ideas & Inspiration," "Tasks & Techniques," and "Plant Guide."

Each richly illustrated garden plan in the "Garden Ideas & Inspiration" section is accompanied by detailed call-outs of the featured plants and foolproof, step-by-step instructions for creating vibrant, easy-care planting schemes.

With an at-a-glance chart of plant alternatives included in each plan, you can customize designs to reflect your own personal tastes.

In the "Tasks & Techniques" chapter, you'll quickly learn how to turn an ordinary, overgrown or uninspired landscape into a garden filled with perennial delights. Full-color photographs, professional shortcuts, troubleshooting advice and clear, easy-to-follow steps handhold you through each garden project.

The "Plant Guide" section provides detailed information about how and when to purchase plants, as well as hints and tips for incorporating them into your dream designs.

To help you select the best plants for your perennial garden, simply refer to the Zone Map on the inside cover. The map is easy to use: Simply locate the zone in which you live, and then choose plants listed for that zone. Zonal information can be found in the "Best Conditions" box on the front of each gatefold Plant Guide.

from seed to bloom: starting perennials from the ground up

PERENNIAL GARDENING IS AN ART THAT ALLOWS YOU TO CREATIVELY reflect your personal tastes on a living canvas. Whether you want to dabble with spring's soothing palette of pastels for a cottage-garden masterpiece or compose a symphony of wildflowers with a concert of sun-splashed hues, your final composition should always have your special signature on it. To help you define your own personal style, *Perennials for Sun* showcases bright, beautiful planting schemes that will spark your imagination, as well as plant alternatives for tailoring each design idea to your liking. Simply mix and match this volume's featured perennials to create a garden that complements the color and style of your home and, most importantly, your love for flowers.

For a stunning tide of color that comes back faithfully each season, choose the wide range of hues, sizes and shapes that perennials—plants that continue to bloom year after year—have to offer. Planting a bed with these flowers saves you time spent digging up and planting new flowers each year and money spent on flowers that only survive for one season. To ensure a long-lasting show in your garden, check seed packets and tags on nursery plants to find those with the longest bloom times.

When you buy plants marked "full sun," it's important to understand exactly what that term implies. In general, plants that require full sun should receive at least six hours of direct sun a day. To increase light in a specific area, prune overhanging tree limbs that may block the sun's rays. Alternatively, you can use white pebbles in a nearby pathway to reflect light onto your plants, or use white paint on a wall adjacent to your garden to attract light to corners.

Plants grow best and reach their full potential when their requirements match the site conditions in which they're growing. Before choosing sun-loving perennials for your garden, first evaluate your landscape, identifying sun and shade patterns and the varying soil conditions in your yard. Then, using this volume's

pick the best plants for your site

Starting a perennial garden from seeds is an inexpensive way to enjoy a diverse mix of plant colors and varieties. Seed packets not only offer an economical source of plant material but also provide you with a practical way to grow mass plantings of the same color and type of plant.

Observing and nurturing a tiny seedling as it grows into a majestic blooming plant is a rewarding and satisfying experience. Creating a garden with perennial seeds is an exciting process—one that puts you in touch with the rhythms of the seasons.

"Garden Ideas & Inspiration" section, map out your planting scheme based on these features. Once they're planted, if you find that the sun and soil needs of newly established perennials aren't being met, simply move them to a new site where they will flourish.

Buying perennials as plants is a quick way to add instant color to the garden. You can either order plants through mail-order catalogs or visit your local nursery and bring plants home the very same day. Most gardeners will use both catalogs and garden centers to take advantage of the benefits that each has to offer.

Plants sent via mail are often shipped bareroot in a dormant state, so keep in mind that they may not look like much when they arrive and will need to be planted as soon as possible. If you won't be home the moment the order arrives, arrange for a protected site—away from heat or cold—where the box of live plants can be stored.

If you're an impatient gardener, buying plants from a nursery gives instant gratification and often yields larger plants. The selection may not be as broad and you may pay more for mature plants in gallon containers, but you won't have to wait as long for a big show once they're set in the ground.

Getting to know the local nursery folks is another advantage to shopping locally. You won't have to worry about taking home plants that won't survive in your climate, and you'll get instant answers to your growing questions at the check-out counter.

a sitting garden

GARDEN IDEAS & INSPIRATION

Ideas for a
Fall Color Flower Border

Add spice to a sunny border by planting
dazzling flowers to bloom against
the warm shades of autumn.

The Best of Autumn's Shades

Make the most of golden sunshine in fall by growing a wealth of colorful flowers for cutting.

Plant this lovely border in spring, lining a path or the lawn, so you can appreciate a profusion of colorful blooms while taking a stroll through the garden in autumn.

This fall-flowering border only requires average soil, and sun or light shade. A few tall growers, however, may need staking once they begin to grow.

**BUGBANE
(CIMICIFUGA RACEMOSA)**
H: 5 ft., S: 2 ft.; pure white, feathery flower spikes; needs staking; zones 3-8

NEW ENGLAND ASTER
H: 4-5 ft., S: 2 ft.; pyramid-shaped clusters of large pink-violet blooms; good for cut flowers; full sun or light shade; zones 5-8

PENSTEMON
H: 1-3 ft., S: 3-4 ft.; tubular, red flowers; needs moisture; full sun or light shade; zones 6-8

PHYGELIUS AEQUALIS
H and S: 2 ft.; cream-yellow flower clusters; dig up and store in winter; zones 7-9

POLYGONUM BISTORTA
H and S: 2 ft.; spikes of pink or rose flowers in summer; zones 4-8

SEDUM 'AUTUMN JOY'
H and S: 18-24 in.;
wine red flowers;
attracts butterflies and
bees; zones 4-9

COREOPSIS 'GOLDEN CROWN'
H: 30 in., S: 8 in.;
full sun; good cut
flower; annual;
all zones

LADY'S-MANTLE
H: 9-12 in., S: 24 in.;
yellow-green flowers
in late spring; zones 4-8

1 **Use a hose** to lay out the curving front edge of the border. Cut out the front of the border with a half-moon edger.

2 **Plant three Asters** at the back left of border with 4 ft. stakes. To the right, 5 ft. away from Asters, plant three Bugbanes with stakes.

3 **Plant five** Sedums in front of Bugbanes, and three Penstemons to left of Asters. Plant *Polygonum bistorta* to left of Penstemons.

4 **At the front** of the border, plant trios of Lady's-mantle, Coreopsis, and *Phygelius aequalis*. Space these clusters 12 in. apart.

5 **As Asters** and Bugbanes grow, tie them loosely to stakes with thin twine. Water every seven rainless days and deadhead throughout fall.

6 **After blooming** has stopped, cut back long, dead stems. Mulch for winter. For spring color, plant bulbs in foreground of the border.

Ideas for a Fall Color Flower Border

More Plants for Fall Color

AREAS		PLANT	DESCRIPTION
BORDERS		Winter Daffodil *(far left)*	Crocus-like, yellow flowers; gray-green leaves; 6 in.; zones 6-9
		Cyclamen (left) neapolitanum	White or pink blooms; Ivy-shaped, silvery leaves; 4 in.; zones 5-9
		Colchicum	Reddish purple, pink, or white funnel-like blooms; 8 in.; zones 4-9
		Merendera montana	Deep rose or violet funnel-shaped blooms; 2 in.; zones 6-9
FOREGROUND		Helenium *(far left)*	Gold- or red-fringed flowers with brown centers; 24-30 in.; zones 6-9
		Miscanthus 'Aureola' *(left)*	Spiky, light green leaves turn brown in fall; 16 in.; zones 5-9
		Nerine	White, pink, or red blooms; slender stalks; 2 ft.; zones 8-10
		Heather *(Calluna)*	White, pink, or purple blooms; late summer or fall; 9-24 in.; zones 5-8
MIDDLE GROUND		Red Turtlehead *(far left)*	Spikes of hooded, fuchsia flowers; deep green leaves; 3 ft.; zones 5-9
		Chrysanthemum *(left)*	Yellow, red, orange, white, or purple blooms; 2-5 ft.; zones 5-9
		Salvia 'Bethellii'	Sub-shrub perennial; long, cerise-red, tubular blooms; 5 ft.; zones 7-9
		Chinese Plumbago	Blue flowers with white centers; red leaves in fall; 3 ft.; zones 7-10
BACKGROUND		Burning Bush *(far left)*	Dark green leaves turn fiery red in autumn; 5-6 ft.; zones 4-9
		Joe-Pye Weed *(left)*	Tubular, dusty pink flowers on purple stems; 7 ft.; zones 3-10
		Fatsia japonica	Glossy, dark green leaves; white flower spikes; 10 ft.; zones 8-10
		Berberis 'Rubrostilla'	Gray-green foliage turns bright red in fall; red berries; 5 ft.; zones 7-9

Ideas for a
Classic Perennial Garden

*To create a unified parade of color,
plant perennials in clumps and repeat the
arrangement the length of the garden.*

Jewel-like Colors that Last for Years

Repeating clumps of color along a perennial border helps unify the design and creates a garden that delights the eye.

This classic perennial border features Poppies, Lupines, and other perennials that create masses of stunning color in late spring to early summer. The design features several colors, and the plants are arranged in groups of three to five per clump. Because the flowers bloom in large clusters, they produce areas of color that are dramatic even from a distance. Repeating colors along the length of the border creates a picture that is visually unified.

For a vibrant border that is filled with color from spring to fall, plant a variety of perennials that bloom in different seasons.

LUPINE
H: 3-4 ft., S: 2 ft.; upright spikes of pink, red, white, or purple flowers in early summer; compound leaves; prefers cool summers; zones 3-8

LAMB'S-EARS
H: 6-15 in., S: 2 ft.; fuzzy spikes of tiny, pinkish purple flowers in summer; evergreen, woolly, silver leaves; zones 4-9

BETHLEHEM SAGE
H: 1 ft., S: 1 ½-2 ft.; clusters of pink buds open to blue flowers in early spring; attractive, long, pointed, green foliage spotted with silver; prefers partial to full shade; zones 3-8

DIANTHUS
H: 10 in., S: 2 ft.; masses of spice-scented, pink, red, or white flowers in late spring to early summer; blue-green, evergreen foliage; zones 4-8

SWEET WILLIAM
H: 6-18 in., S: 8-12 in.; flat-topped clusters of fragrant, red, pink, or white flowers in early summer; narrow, dark green leaves; reseeding biennial or short-lived perennial; zones 3-9

ORIENTAL POPPY
H: 2-3 ft., S: 3 ft.;
large, orange, red-
orange, red, salmon,
pink, or white blooms
with black centers in
early summer; foliage
disappears after plants
flower; zones 2-7

1 **Clear weeds** and debris from a site 5 ft. wide and 20 ft. long. Spread a 2 in. layer of compost and dig it in to a depth of at least 12 in.

2 **Plant three clumps** of Oriental Poppies, one at either end of the border and one in the center. Space three plants 2 ft. apart in the clump.

3 **Plant two clumps** of five Lupines, 1 ft. apart, between the Poppies. Plant a clump of three Lamb's-ears at center of garden, 1 ft. apart.

4 **Fill in the front** of the border with Dianthus, *Viola cornutas*, Bethlehem Sages, and Sweet Williams. Space all plants 1 ft. apart.

5 **In early summer**, after the Poppies have finished blooming and their foliage disappears, plant Marigolds or other annuals in empty site.

6 **In late summer** or the following spring, add clumps of other perennials that bloom in summer and fall to create an extended display.

VIOLA CORNUTA
'LUTEA SPLENDENS'
H and S: 8-10 in.; bright
yellow, Pansy-like flowers
all summer; heart-shaped
leaves; zones 5-9

More Plants for a Classic Perennial Garden

COLOR	PLANT	DESCRIPTION
RED & PINK	Gas Plant 'Ruber' *(far left)*	Fragrant, pale pink summer flowers; compound leaves; 1-4 ft.; zones 3-8
	Crocosmia 'Lucifer' *(left)*	Flame-red flowers in midsummer; narrow leaves; 3 ½ ft.; zones 5-9
	Gayfeather 'Kobold'	Fluffy, lilac-pink spikes in summer; narrow leaves; 2 ½ ft.; zones 3-9
	Peony 'Buckeye Belle'	Dark red blooms in late spring; dark green leaves; 3 ft.; zones 2-8
YELLOW & ORANGE	Heliopsis 'Golden Plume' *(far left)*	Double, gold summer flowers; dark green leaves; 3 ft.; zones 3-9
	Daylily 'Witch Hazel' *(left)*	Yellow-orange summer blooms; slender leaves; 1 ½ ft.; zones 3-9
	Lily 'Anaconda'	Fragrant, apricot summer trumpets; narrow leaves; 6 ft.; zones 5-8
	Centaurea macrocephala	Yellow, Thistle-like flowers; lance-like leaves; 4 ft.; zones 2-8
BLUE & PURPLE	Blue Flax *(far left)*	Sky blue summer flowers; needle-like leaves; 1 ½ ft.; zones 4-9
	Campanula lactiflora (left)	Violet-blue flowers in summer; deeply cut leaves; 1 ½ ft.; zones 4-8
	Geranium x magnificum	Deep purple blooms in late spring; lobed leaves; 3 ft.; zones 3-9
	Delphinium 'King Arthur'	Blue or white flowers in summer; lobed leaves; 4 ft.; zones 3-8
WHITE	Veronica 'Icicle' *(far left)*	Spikes of white summer flowers; lance-like leaves; 3 ft.; zones 3-8
	Peony 'Krinkled White' *(left)*	White-and-gold late spring blooms; dark green leaves; 3 ft.; zones 2-8
	Bearded Iris 'Leda's Lover'	White late spring blooms; sword-shaped leaves; 3 ft.; zones 3-9
	Baby's Breath 'Perfecta'	Clouds of white flowers in summer; dark green leaves; 3 ft.; zones 3-9

Ideas for Waves of
Early Summer Color

*Transform a sunny site with sweeps of
eye-catching color by planting masses of flowers
in a flowing design.*

Bountiful, Bold Blooms

Planting flowers in drifts or waves increases the impact of the blooms by creating brilliant blocks of color.

Masses of colorful blooms make an exciting display in any garden, and this one is no exception. It is planted with perennials in clumps of three to five plants to create bold blocks of color for an eye-catching design.

All the plants in this garden thrive with full sun and rich soil that is evenly moist and well drained. It is planted in two stages: Peonies and Oriental Poppies are planted in the fall, while the rest of the flowers are planted in spring.

DELPHINIUM
H: 2-7 ft.,
S: 2 ft.; blue,
lilac, or white
flower spikes in
late spring to early
summer; needs
staking; prefers cool
conditions; zones 3-7

SIBERIAN IRIS
H: 3 ft., S: 4 ft.;
blue, purple, white, yellow, or
bicolored flowers from late spring
to early summer; forms clumps of
attractive, sword-shaped leaves;
grows well in wet soil; zones 2-9

PEONY
H: 2-3 ft., S: 3 ft.;
fragrant, pink, white, or
crimson flowers from late
spring to early summer;
attractive, dark green foliage
all summer; zones 3-8

SHASTA DAISY
H: 2-3 ft., S: 2 ft.;
white, single or
double Daisies with
yellow centers in
summer; requires
well-drained soil;
zones 4-9

ORIENTAL POPPY
H: 2-3 ft., S: 3 ft.;
large, orange, red-
orange, red, salmon,
pink, or white blooms
with black centers in
early summer; foliage
disappears after
flowering; zones 2-7

1 Mark off a bed at least 20 ft. by 6 ft. with stakes and string. Remove grass, spread 3 in. of compost, and dig site to a shovel's depth.

2 In spring, space the Siberian Irises 2 ft. apart, and the Delphiniums and Shasta Daisies 1 ft. apart. Mulch to control weeds.

3 Plant the Poppies in fall. Space plants 1 ½ ft. apart. Handle Poppies with great care, as the roots are very brittle.

4 Plant bareroot Peonies in fall. Buds must be only 1-2 in. below the soil surface. Peonies planted too deeply will not bloom.

5 Keep Delphinium flowers from flopping by staking each stem. Use three stakes for Peony clumps. Tie stems to stakes with string.

6 Deadhead Poppies when faded. Consider planting annuals, such as Marigolds, to provide color when Poppies finish blooming.

Ideas for Waves of **Early Summer Color**

More Early Summer Bloomers

COLORS	PLANT	DESCRIPTION
RED & PINK	Painted Daisy *(far left)*	Pink blooms with gold centers; Fern-like foliage; 2 ft.; zones 3-7
	Red Valerian *(left)*	Tall, reddish pink flowers; blue-green leaves; 1-3 ft.; zones 4-8
	Bearded Penstemon	Pink to red blooms; tall stems; oval leaves; 2-3 ft.; zones 3-8
	Astilbe 'Venus'	Pink, plume-like flowers; serrated leaflets; 2-4 ft.; zones 3-9
WHITE	Gas Plant *(far left)*	White or pink flowers from late spring to summer; 1-4 ft.; zones 3-8
	Willow Bellflower *(left)*	Pure white, bell-shaped flowers all summer; 1-3 ft.; zones 4-8
	Carolina Phlox 'Miss Lingard'	White flowers from summer to fall; dark green leaves; 3 ft.; zones 3-9
	White False Indigo	Spikes of white, Pea-like flowers; gray-green foliage; 2-3 ft.; zones 5-8
BLUE & PURPLE	Blue False Indigo *(far left)*	Spikes of lavender-blue flowers; gray-green foliage; 2-4 ft.; zones 3-9
	Bugloss *(left)*	Bright blue flower spikes; hairy stems and leaves; 2-5 ft.; zones 3-8
	Giant Onion	Globe-shaped, 5 in. balls of purple flowers; 3-5 ft.; zones 4-8
	Spiny Bear's Breech	Purple and white flowers on spikes; spiny leaves; 3-4 ft.; zones 7-10
YELLOW & ORANGE	Asiatic Hybrid Lily *(far left)*	Orange, yellow, red, white, or pink flowers; 3-4 ft.; zones 4-8
	Yarrow 'Moonshine' *(left)*	Sulphur yellow flower clusters; Fern-like leaves; 2 ft.; zones 3-8
	Blackberry Lily	Orange flowers and Blackberry-like seeds; 2-4 ft.; zones 4-10
	Carolina Lupine	Spikes of yellow flowers; gray-green foliage; 3-5 ft.; zones 3-9

Ideas for a Pale
Summer Perennial Bed

Create an elegant, peaceful garden by combining perennials with pastel blooms and using distinctive, easy-to-grow foliage plants as accents.

A Cool Pastel Parade

For a summer-long succession of flowers, plant long-blooming perennials and give them full sun and rich soil.

Perennials with pastel pink, white, or blue flowers create lacy clouds of blooms in this elegant bed. Planting in clumps of two or more ensures that the delicately hued flowers will create a bold visual effect. Clumps are arranged by height. A dark fence sets off the tallest perennials, which in turn provide a backdrop for lower-growing flowers. The blue-green leaves of Blue Oat Grass add texture and season-long color to the design.

A site in full sun and rich, well-drained soil will ensure healthy growth and encourage a long season of blooms.

ROSE CAMPION 'ALBA'
H: 1 ½-2 ft., S: 1 ½ ft.: branched clusters of white flowers from mid- to late summer; woolly, silver-gray stems and leaves; zones 4-8

BLUE OAT GRASS (*HELICTOTRICHON SEMPERVIRENS*)
H: 1-1 ½ ft., S: 1 ½-2 ft.; Oat-like seedheads in summer; dense clumps of blue-green, evergreen leaves; zones 4-9

PENSTEMON 'PINK BEAUTY'
H: 2-2 ½ ft., S: 1 ft.; spikes of two-lipped, pink flowers from summer to early fall; lance-like, gray-green leaves; zones 3-8

LAVATERA THURINGIACA 'BARNSLEY'
H: 5-6 ft., S: 4-5 ft.; spikes of trumpet-shaped flowers in summer that open white and fade to pink; rounded, lobed leaves; zones 8-10; grown as an annual in the North

1 **Remove lawngrass** and weeds from a 6 ft. wide by 8 ft. long site. Work a 2 in. layer of compost deeply into the soil.

2 **In early spring,** as soon as soil can be worked, rake a smooth seedbed at front of the bed. Sow Chinese Forget-me-not seeds.

3 **Plant *Lavatera thuringiaca*** centered in the back of the garden. Plant three Penstemons 1 ft. apart directly in front of *Lavatera*.

4 **Plant three** Rose Campions 2 ½ ft. back from front of bed. Space 1 ft. apart. Plant Blue Oat Grass 1 ft. from front edge.

CHINESE FORGET-ME-NOTS
H: 1 ½ ft., S: 1 ft.; loose clusters of pure blue flowers from late spring through summer; woolly, gray-green leaves; annual; all zones

5 **Remove faded flowers** from Rose Campions to encourage new blooms. Leave a few flowers to form seeds for self-sowing.

6 **In zones 4-7** in summer, take cuttings of *Lavatera*. Root cuttings in vermiculite and pot them up. Overwinter plants indoors.

25

Ideas for a Pale **Summer Perennial Bed**

More Pale Summer Perennials

TYPE			PLANT	DESCRIPTION
SHORT			*Allium senescens (far left)*	Rosy lilac flowers in summer; grass-like leaves; 1 ft.; zones 3-9
			Baby's Breath 'Rosea' *(left)*	Small, pink flowers in summer; tiny leaves; 8 in.; zones 3-8
			Columbine 'Corbette'	Yellow flowers in early summer; blue-green leaves; 1 ft.; zones 3-9
			Alchemilla alpina	Yellow-green summer flowers; lobed leaves; 8 in.; zones 3-7
MEDIUM			Willow Blue Star *(far left)*	Starry, pale blue late spring flowers; narrow leaves; 2 ft.; zones 3-9
			Daylily 'Catherine Woodbury' *(left)*	Pale pink summer trumpets; strap-like leaves; 2 ½ ft.; zones 3-9
			Cupid's-dart	Blue, Daisy-like summer flowers; gray-green leaves; 2 ft.; zones 5-8
			Achillea 'Rose Beauty'	Flat, rose pink clusters in summer; Fern-like leaves; 2 ft.; zones 3-8
TALL			Phlox 'Bright Eyes' *(far left)*	Pink summer blooms with darker eyes; narrow leaves; 4 ft.; zones 3-8
			Queen-of-the-prairie *(left)*	Fluffy, pink summer flowers; dark green leaves; 6 ft.; zones 3-9
			Bellflower 'Grandiflora'	Cupped, lilac blue summer flowers; narrow leaves; 3 ft.; zones 4-8
			Jupiter's Beard	Rose red flowers in early summer; blue-green leaves; 3 ft.; zones 4-8
FOLIAGE FILLERS			Fescue 'Elija Blue' *(far left)*	Silver-blue, evergreen foliage; lacy seedheads; 10 in.; zones 4-8
			Fountain Grass 'Hamelin' *(left)*	Clumps of narrow, arching leaves; white seedheads; 1 ft.; zones 5-10
			Coral Bells 'Ruby Ruffles'	Wine-and-silver leaves; tiny, white summer flowers; 1 ft.; zones 4-9
			Artemisia 'Lambrook Silver'	Lacy, silver-gray foliage; tiny, gold summer flowers; 3 ft.; zones 4-9

Designs for a Bed of
Daisy-Like Blooms

For a bounty of carefree, country-style summer color, plant drifts of Daisy-like flowers highlighted by a few flowers offering different shapes.

Cheerful, Easy Summer Color

For an effective display, arrange plants in natural-looking clumps, mixing Daisy-like blooms with contrasting flowers.

Daisy-like blooms have irresistible charm that adds welcome color and appeal to any style of planting, from formal perennial borders to small, informal flower beds. This garden, which is overflowing with Daisies in all colors, has a casual, country-style design. Mass plantings of Daisies create a ribbon of color across the landscape. They are combined with flowers in contrasting shapes as well as ornamental grasses to create a natural, meadow-like look.

All of the plants in this garden thrive in full sun and in average to rich, well-drained soil.

QUEEN ANNE'S LACE
H: 2-3 ft., S: 1-1 ½ ft.; lacy, flat-topped, white flower clusters in summer; finely divided, Fern-like leaves; annual or biennial; zones 3-10

RUDBECKIA HIRTA 'BLACK-EYED SUSAN MIX'
H: 2 ½-3 ft., S: 1 ft.; showy summer flowers with black-brown centers and petals in a mix of orange-yellow, maroon, or red-brown; lance-like leaves; short-lived perennial grown as an annual; all zones

COREOPSIS 'MOONBEAM'
H: 1 ½-2 ft., S: 1 ft.; dainty, pale yellow Daisies from summer to fall; lacy, dark green leaves; zones 4-9

DAYLILIES
H: 1-4 ft., S: 1 ½-3 ft.; trumpet-shaped summer flowers in every color except blue; strap-like leaves; zones 3-9

PURPLE CONEFLOWER
H: 4 ft., S: 1 ½-2 ft.; pink summer Daisies with orange-brown, cone-like centers; lance-like leaves; zones 4-9

SHASTA DAISY
H: 2-3 ft., S: 2 ft.;
white, single or
double Daisies in
summer with yellow
centers; dark green
leaves; zones 4-9

BLUE OAT GRASS
H and S: 1-1 ½ ft.;
ornamental grass with
clumps of arching,
blue-green leaves; tan
seedheads above foliage in
early summer; zones 4-9

1 **Sow *Rudbeckia* seeds** in pots indoors in late winter. In spring, as soon as ground can be worked, clear a 10 ft. by 5 ft. area of grass.

2 **Loosen soil** to 1 ft. Set *Rudbeckia* seedlings outdoors in a sheltered spot for one week to harden off before transplanting them.

3 **Plant *Rudbeckia*** 1 ft. apart in a wavy-edged band across garden. Plant Coneflowers, Daylilies, and Shasta Daisies 2 ft. apart.

4 **Plant Blue Oat Grass,** Coreopsis, and Queen Anne's Lace along edges of the band of *Rudbeckia*. Space all plants 1 ft. apart.

5 **Let *Rudbeckia* flowers** set seed. In fall, crumble seedheads in your hand and sprinkle over the garden to encourage reseeding.

6 **In spring,** plant extra *Rudbeckia* seedlings to ensure a thick band of color. Pull up plants near Coreopsis to give it room to grow.

More Plants for a Bed of Daisy-like Blooms

TYPE		PLANT	DESCRIPTION
TALL		Helenium *(far left)*	Red or gold late summer Daisies; lance-like leaves; 3 ft.; zones 3-8
		Cosmos 'Sensation' *(left)*	Pink, red, or white summer blooms; lacy leaves; 3 ft.; annual; all zones
		Coneflower 'White Swan'	White summer Daisies; lance-like leaves; 4 ft.; zones 3-8
		Sunflower 'Aztec Gold'	Golden summer flowers; large leaves; 6 ft.; annual; all zones
MEDIUM		Aster 'Purple Dome' *(far left)*	Purple late summer to fall Daisies; narrow leaves; 2 ft.; zones 3-8
		Painted Daisy *(left)*	Pink, white, or red summer Daisies; Fern-like leaves; 2 ft.; zones 3-7
		Fleabane 'Azure Fairy'	Purple Daisies from summer to fall; lance-like leaves; 18 in.; zones 4-10
		Gerbera 'California Mix'	Orange or pink summer Daisies; large leaves; 2 ft.; annual; all zones
SHORT		Gazania 'Piñata Mix' *(far left)*	Orange or red summer blooms; silver leaves; 1 ft.; annual; all zones
		Hardy Ice Plant *(left)*	Purple Daisies all summer; fleshy, green leaves; 5 in.; zones 6-9
		Zinnia 'Starbright Mix'	Orange or white summer Daisies; thin leaves; 8 in.; annual; all zones
		Blue Marguerite 'Cub Scout'	Blue summer to fall Daisies; oval leaves; 6 in.; annual; all zones
CONTRASTING FLOWERS		Cleome 'Rose Queen' *(far left)*	Spidery, rose pink flowers; narrow leaves; 4 ft.; annual; all zones
		Phlox 'Miss Lingard' *(left)*	White summer to early fall flowers; oval leaves; 3 ft.; zones 3-9
		Liatris ligulistylis	Spikes of pink summer flowers; grass-like leaves; 5 ft.; zones 3-9
		Purple Fountain Grass	Red summer flower spikes; purple leaves; 2-3 ft.; annual; all zones

Ideas for Planting a
Sea of Summer Pinks

*Plant waves of color along a border in hues from
pale to shocking pink by arranging masses of
summer-blooming flowers in free-form shapes.*

Variations on a Single Color

Create an unforgettable show by planting pink-flowered perennials in a variety of hues, shapes, and textures.

A foolproof way to create a garden color scheme is to start with a color you love. For best results, mix a variety of shades and hues. This garden, for example, features rosy pink Coneflowers, purple-pink Spiderworts, and a variety of harmonizing flowers in hues from palest pink to red. A splash of blue or purple intensifies the pinks. Include different flower and leaf shapes and textures to add even more interest.

Extend the display by choosing flowers with a range of blooming seasons, from early to late summer. All the flowers in this border thrive in full sun and rich, well-drained soil.

GERANIUM 'JOHNSON'S BLUE'
H and S: 16-18 in.; mounds of five-petaled, clear blue flowers from early to late summer; deeply divided, lacy leaves; zones 4-8

OBEDIENT PLANT
H: 3-4 ft., S: 4-5 ft.; small, two-lipped, pink flowers in late summer; lance-like leaves; vigorous spreader; individual flowers are "hinged" and can be pointed in any direction on the stalk; zones 3-9

PURPLE CONEFLOWER 'MAGNUS'
H: 2-4 ft., S: 3-4 ft.; large, flattened, Daisy-like flowers in summer with rosy pink petals and orange-brown centers; lance-like leaves; zones 3-8

SPIDERWORT 'PAULINE'
H: 1-2 ft., S: 3-4 ft.; small, purplish pink flowers in early summer that open for only half a day; strap-like leaves; vigorous spreader; cut plants to ground in midsummer and new foliage will emerge; zones 3-9

CARDINAL FLOWER
H: 2-4 ft., S: 1-2 ft.;
spikes of flame red
flowers in summer and
fall; lance-like
leaves; zones 2-9

**YARROW 'SUMMER
PASTELS MIXED'**
H: 2 ft., S: 2-3 ft.; flat-
topped summer
clusters of tiny flowers
in pale mauve, rust,
salmon, cream,
yellow, or lilac; Fern-
like, fragrant
leaves; zones 3-9

**HELENIUM
'CRIMSON BEAUTY'**
H and S: 2 ½-4 ft.;
mahogany red, Daisy-like
flowers with button-like
centers from late summer
to fall; lance-like leaves;
zones 3-8

1 **Clear all weeds** and lawngrass from a 12 ft. by 4 ft. site. Spread 3 in. of compost and loosen the soil to a depth of 12 in.

2 **Use a long stick** to draw free-form planting areas in the soil to create a wave-like design. Plant Purple Coneflowers 3 ft. apart.

3 **Plant the Geraniums** 18 in. apart next to Purple Coneflowers. Plant Spiderworts and Heleniums 3 ft. apart along front of bed.

4 **Plant Obedient Plants** 4 ft. apart at the back of border. Fill in back of bed with Yarrows 2 ft. apart and Cardinal Flowers 1 ft. apart.

5 **Cut Spiderworts** to the ground when they begin to stop blooming and the foliage gets ragged. Fresh foliage will regrow quickly.

6 **Dig up and divide** Purple Coneflowers, Obedient Plants, Spiderworts, and Yarrows every two years to contain spreading.

33

More Plants for a Sea of Summer Pinks

TYPE	PLANT	DESCRIPTION
LOW PERENNIALS	Pink Coreopsis *(far left)*	Pink, Daisy-like blooms; thread-like leaves; 12-15 in.; zones 3-9
	Ajuga 'Burgundy Glow' *(left)*	Blue flowers; pink, purple, white, and green foliage; 5 in.; zones 3-9
	Thrift 'Vindictive'	Globe-shaped, rose red flowers; grass-like leaves; 6 in.; zones 3-8
	Dianthus x alwoodii 'Mars'	Fragrant, double, pink blooms; evergreen leaves; 6 in.; zones 5-8
MEDIUM PERENNIALS	Painted Daisy *(far left)*	Pink, rose, or red, yellow-centered Daisies; lacy leaves; 2 ft.; zones 3-7
	Baby's Breath 'Pink Fairy' *(left)*	Mounds of double, pink flowers; dark green leaves; 2 ft.; zones 3-9
	Astilbe 'Hyacinth'	Lilac-rose flower plumes; green, Fern-like foliage; 2 ft.; zones 3-9
	Anemone 'Margarete'	Deep pink, semi-double blooms; dark green leaves; 3 ft.; zones 5-8
TALL PERENNIALS	Aster 'Barr's Pink' *(far left)*	Magenta, Daisy-like blooms; narrow leaves; 3 ft.; zones 3-8
	Gladiolus communis (left)	Orchid-like, deep pink flowers; strap-like leaves; 3 ft.; zones 6-10
	Giant Allium 'Globemaster'	Round, rosy purple flowers; strap-like leaves; 3-5 ft.; bulb; zones 4-8
	Meadowsweet 'Venusta'	Fluffy, deep rose flowers; deeply cut leaves; 4-6 ft.; zones 3-9
ANNUALS	Lavatera 'Silver Cup' *(far left)*	Pink, flattened, trumpet-like blooms; Maple-like leaves; 2 ft.; all zones
	Annual Phlox 'Carnival' *(left)*	Bicolored blooms in many hues; lance-like leaves; 6 in.; all zones
	Cleome 'Color Fountain Mix'	Pink, rose, purple, or white flowers; narrow leaves; 4 ft.; all zones
	Nicotiana 'Domino Pink'	Sweetly scented, salmon-pink blooms; oval leaves; 1 ft.; all zones

TASKS & TECHNIQUES

A Guide to Preparing a
New Garden Site

Get your garden off to the best possible start by preparing the site before you plant.

PREPARING A NEW FLOWER GARDEN SITE

YOU WILL NEED:

- ❏ Shovel
- ❏ Stakes and string
- ❏ Rake
- ❏ Organic material
- ❏ Granular fertilizer
- ❏ Border edging

Tip

Healthy soil is the key to a successful garden so before you prepare the site, have a soil sample evaluated by a soil lab. The test results will tell you which amendments will do the most for your particular conditions and which to avoid adding.

1 Select and stake a garden site. Mark off the outline of the garden by digging a trench around the edge, or by using stakes and string.

2 Clear the area of weeds and debris and add a thick layer of organic material such as well-rotted manure, leaf mold, compost, or humus.

3 Add fertilizer. Sprinkle a complete granular fertilizer over the entire bed, following rates recommended on the label. Mix in well.

4 Rake the bed smooth, removing any rocks that surface. Add any paths and a border to give a finished look and help keep soil in place.

PREPARING A NEW VEGETABLE GARDEN SITE

YOU WILL NEED: ❏ Spade ❏ Rake ❏ Tiller ❏ Organic materials ❏ Granular fertilizer

1 Remove weeds and rocks from garden site. If necessary, use a spade to remove existing turf.

2 Spread a thick layer of compost or aged manure and granular fertilizer over the site and till in.

3 Rake the area smooth and form furrows for row plantings or build mounds with basins. Lay stones for a path.

Secrets of Success

Simple but effective steps taken before you plant will yield fantastic results as your garden matures.

WHY PREPARE A NEW SITE?

Grow the best-tasting vegetables and the biggest and brightest flowers by thoroughly preparing the garden site before you plant. A well-prepared site allows plants to establish quickly, put out good roots, and grow strong to resist pests and diseases naturally. The procedures are the same whether you are starting from scratch, expanding the size of an existing bed, or adding a bed in a new spot.

WHEN TO PREPARE A NEW SITE

Ideally, you will want to prepare your site a few seasons before planting, but even several weeks will do. This gives soil amendments plenty of time to start

Well-prepared soil ensures success with new plantings

breaking down, enriching the soil and improving drainage or water retention.

If you cannot plan that far ahead, your garden will still benefit from some preparation immediately before planting. Just be sure to use fully aged manures and compost, as these are already broken down.

HOW TO PREPARE A NEW SITE

Begin by planning. The site should be large enough and provide the appropriate conditions for the plants you wish to grow. Site conditions include sun exposure, soil type, shelter from wind, and water availability. For instance, rock gardens do best with well-drained soil and full sun; vegetable gardens need rich soil, full sun, and lots of water; herb

gardens do best with poor to average soil, full sun, and less water. Mark off site and remove weeds, debris, rocks, and any overhanging limbs.

The most important aspect is soil preparation. Mixing in organic material, such as compost or manure, boosts fertility, helps sandy soils retain water and nutrients, and also improves drainage for heavy, clay soils. Finish by edging the bed or adding pathways for easy access when harvesting.

If you have a rototiller, you may be tempted to turn under sod rather than removing it. But grass will sprout even if turned under, so removing all turf before planting is a better idea.

Be sure to amend soil

A Guide to Preparing a New Garden Site

Seasonal Tips

Once the soil has been worked and the bed is edged and in final form, water the area over several days and wait for the weeds to sprout. Then, with a minimum of trampling, pull all the small weeds. This saves work later when the garden is planted, especially if you plant seeds.

FALL
Preparing
Plan your spring garden and, if possible, prepare the site before winter sets in *(above)*. This will give the organic materials in the soil plenty of time to begin breaking down.

SPRING
Preparing & Sowing
If you did not prepare your bed in fall, start preparing it as soon as the ground thaws and dries out a bit (about the same time you start sowing most seeds indoors).

SUMMER
Maintaining
If plants do not appear to be growing well, test your soil and adjust by adding soil amendments as needed.

Weather Watch

If recent rains have made the soil soggy, hold off on preparing your planting site. You can do more harm than good if the soil is sticky and hard to work. Instead, let the soil dry to a crumbly consistency before mixing in any amendments.

Prevent weeds from growing in walkways or between plantings with weed block fabric. This porous, lightweight material stops almost all weeds from sprouting. Lay out and pin fabric down after you have prepared the site. Use a mulch to hide the material.

A Basic Guide to
Staking Flowering Plants

Keep top-heavy, flowering plants standing tall at center stage with simple staking methods.

Standing Long and Strong

Staking flowers helps their blooms last longer and look better.

WHY STAKE FLOWERS?

Plants that produce tall, top-heavy, floppy, or low and spindly flower stalks often need staking to keep flowers upright and producing at peak levels. Flopping stems are easily broken and tend to get less sun. Also, blooms or stems that bend down to touch the ground are an open invitation for pest and disease problems.

In addition to alleviating these problems, staking also helps minimize damage from strong winds and storms and gives the garden a tidy look.

Properly placed, hidden supports disappear among plants

WHAT TO STAKE

Annuals, perennials, and bulbs with flowers on tall or sprawling stems all benefit from staking. Plants that receive excess water and nitrogen may grow leggy and require stake supports, as will plants growing in shady or particularly windy sites.

HOW TO STAKE

The type of stake you use depends primarily on the growth habit of the plant being staked.

Single bamboo or metal stakes work well when positioned next to plants with individual stems, such as Tulips or Cosmos. The plant stem should be loosely fastened to the stake with raffia or soft twine.

Metal hoop or cage supports placed over and around plants are ideal for added support to mid-sized plants with multiple stems, such as Heleniums, Peonies, or Purple Coneflowers.

Wire cages are used to support very tall plants with multiple stems, such as Rudbeckias or Hollyhocks.

Lightweight plants, such as Baby's Breath, can be staked by surrounding them with a string around three stakes or using short, well-branched twigs.

Regardless of the method used, all plants should be staked at sowing time or when new growth shows. Stakes should be tall enough to reach just below the flowers at maturity. Try to keep supports hidden among foliage or behind stems so they do not detract from the plant. Or, use green stakes that will blend in with the planting as it matures.

Use stakes for single stems

STAKING WITH CAGES OR HOOPS

Tip

Try to avoid tying plants too tightly to their supports, since the tie may strangle the stem as it matures. As a rule of thumb, you should be able to insert at least one finger between the stem and support when tied. Or better yet, use flexible ties, such as old nylons, to secure plants.

1 **Choose and prepare** a planting site for flowers. Be sure to leave adequate spacing to allow for supports and mature plants.

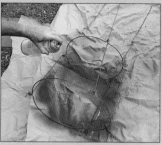

2 **Select a hoop** or cage of appropriate height that will be least obtrusive in the garden. Spray paint the support green if it is not that color.

3 **Insert the cage** or hoop at planting time or, for established perennials, when new growth appears. Place outside the plant's roots.

4 **As plants grow,** wind stems through support or fasten with flexible ties. Check ties as plant matures to make sure they are not too tight.

STAKING WITH SINGLE STAKES

1 **Insert stakes** at least 6 in. deep in prepared soil. Sow seeds or plant bulbs about 1-2 in. from stakes.

2 **When a flower bud** appears on a plant, loosely tie the plant's stem to its stake with a flexible tie.

3 **Check ties periodically** to make sure they are secure, but not tight. Remove stakes when blooms fade.

A Basic Guide to Staking Flowering Plants

Staking Popular Flowers

TYPE	PLANT	METHOD	TIPS
ANNUALS	Cleome	Hoop or stake	Position when plants are 2-3 in. tall; train stems into hoop
	Cosmos (*left*)	Stake	Use stakes to support individual stems of taller varieties
	Sunflower	Stake	Stake only if leaning; needs support in windy areas
	Zinnia	Hoop or stake	Use hoops for tallest stalks and stakes for small ones
PERENNIALS	Baby's Breath	Brush or low hoop	Tuck brush under growth; use hoop for large plants
	Perennial Verbena (*left*)	Hoop or stake	Support stems in windy areas; use hoops on tallest varieties
	Delphinium	Hoop or stake	Use hoops for tall stalks; use stakes for short varieties
	Chrysanthemum	Stake, hoop, or brush	Control small plants with stakes; use hoops for larger plantings
BULBS	Freesia	Hoop or stake	Choose type of support based on the height of variety
	Lily (*left*)	Stake	Support slender stems of taller varieties with stakes
	Gladiolus	Stake	Support each individual flower stalk with a tall stake
	Dahlia	Hoop or stake	Tie to stake when 8-10 in. high; use hoop for large flowers

Seasonal Tips

SPRING
Starting

Start staking process early so you can give complete support to keep flower stalks strong and sturdy. Insert stake so it will just reach to flower level on mature stems. Stake summer-flowering bulbs early.

SUMMER
Adjusting

Adjust new growth to match support as plants mature. Tuck young, supple stems inside wire or string cages before they become tall or brittle. Continue tying single stems to supports as they grow (*right*).

A Guide to Boosting
Perennial Blooms

Follow a few basic steps for years of spectacular blooms from your favorite perennials.

Coaxing More Color

From reliable heirloom plants to new cultivars, well-maintained perennials will give an amazing, long-term floral show.

WHY IMPROVE FLOWERING?

Because perennials are the backbone of flower color in many gardens, improving their blooming will give your landscape a boost and usually improve plant health as well. As long-term plants in the garden, they will produce the best and most flowers if you follow basic, routine care throughout the blooming and growing seasons.

WHEN TO IMPROVE FLOWERING

If your plants have small, weak, or few flowers, or if they look woody with bare centers, it is time for action. Improvement techniques are used at different times, depending on what needs to be done. Some tasks take

Cut back flowers after first bloom to encourage new growth

place before planting, some are ongoing during the growing season, and some are done as growth slows.

HOW TO IMPROVE FLOWERING

Start with excellent soil preparation. Mix in plenty of nutrient-rich amendments, such as compost, well-rotted manure, powdered minerals, and fertilizer. Follow with proper plant selection and placement, so all your perennials will be healthy and vigorous.

Pinch back plants to encourage bushiness and consistently water and weed the garden. It is very important to remove faded flowers so the plant will put out more buds. Stake heavy or sprawling flower stalks early so all stems remain

upright and healthy. Transplant any plants with leggy growth, sunburn, or too little space.

If plants are weak and overcrowded, divide in early spring or just after flowering. This will help rejuvenate plants and give you greater flower production in the seasons to come.

Tip

Fortify plants with a series of doses of liquid fertilizer in the weeks when flowers form. Use a fertilizer that has been designed for flower production in addition to your regular feeding. Apply according to directions.

Transplant to a better place

SIX WAYS TO BETTER FLOWERING PERENNIALS

Make sure soil is balanced with nutrients and organics. Test soil and add manure or compost plus any needed nutrients before planting.

In spring, remove weak stems when they are several inches long. Thinning stems encourages strong, sturdy stems and larger flowers.

Pinch off soft tip growth or side shoots when plant is one-third its final height, so it becomes compact and bushy and bears more flowers.

Deadhead faded flowers during the blooming period to stimulate reblooming types to produce a second round of blooms later on in the season.

Cut back or prune plants by one-half in early spring or after flowering to encourage compact growth that is better for supporting flowers.

Divide old, unproductive plants to rejuvenate them and encourage more flowers by separating with garden forks in early spring or after flowering.

A Guide to Boosting Perennial Blooms

 Seasonal Tips

SPRING
Starting
Start the season off well by amending soil with compost.

SUMMER
Deadheading
Deadhead spent flowers routinely for a continuous show of blossoms *(above)*. Trim wayward, spindly, or dead stems and fertilize.

FALL
Cutting back
Cut back plants after they finish flowering or wait until spring to remove the growth. Cutting back in fall allows you to mulch over plants for winter protection. In mild climates, it produces new growth on which spring flowers flourish.

Weather Watch

In stormy, windy weather, you may have to stake and provide support for tall flowering stalks or cover them temporarily with a sheet of clear plastic so the rain does not destroy their buds or flowers.

AFTERCARE

Most aftercare tasks are simply routine maintenance chores, but they help plants produce more flowers. The most important task is watering newly pruned, fertilized, or divided plants to keep soil evenly moist. Remove competing weeds when they are small so they do not steal needed moisture and nutrients.

Tender new growth and flower buds will be a target for pests and diseases, so be sure to inspect the foliage frequently and take steps to eliminate problems early before a loss occurs. Use traps or collect snails, slugs, and earwigs by hand before they begin to eat flowers and chew leaves.

A Guide to Pruning
Annuals and Perennials

For well-shaped plants with beautiful flowers, use simple methods for controlling growth.

CONTROLLING GROWTH ON PERENNIALS

Tip

For plants that produce good cut flowers, consider cutting the blossoms when they are just before their peak. This will encourage the plant to use its energy to produce more buds instead of seeds, and it allows you to enjoy the flowers indoors. Try Cosmos, Delphiniums, Coneflowers, Coreopsis, and Snapdragons. Cut flowers in the morning or evening, when they have the most moisture.

Remove the outer tips of upward growing stems to encourage bushy side growth. Pinch back early to allow buds the most time to form.

Regularly remove spent flowers so plants do not produce seeds. Cut the stem a few inches down to be sure you get the entire seedpod.

For strong flowering stems, use shears to cut back young shoots on plants that tend to sprawl or become rangy. Cut stems at ground level.

After the first flowering, cut back plants overall by as much as one third. This gives plants good shape and can lead to a second flowering.

CONTROLLING GROWTH ON ANNUALS

Early pinching at planting time helps keep many annuals such as Pansies and Petunias from becoming leggy.

After flowering finishes, cut back tall plants nearly to the ground to encourage a second round of blooms.

Annual vines need only occasional pruning. Shape as needed; remove stems that twine around nearby plants.

Keeping Plants Healthy and Strong

Prolong the blooming period of many of your favorite plants.

WHY PRUNE?

Pruning or thinning your perennials and pinching back annuals improve flowering and keep plants blooming longer. The result is more and sometimes larger flowers. These techniques encourage plants that are healthy and bushy with an abundance of buds early in the season. Later action removes spent flowers for repeat blooming and keeps plants from becoming ragged and overgrown.

WHEN TO PRUNE

Pruning early in the growing season, when the plant has just leafed out, improves shape and removes spindly, weak growth. During the growing season, pruning removes spent flowers, dead growth, and

Deadheading keeps plants neat and encourages more flowers

leggy stems. Late season pruning of perennials eliminates dying stems and prepares plants for winter.

HOW TO PRUNE

With annuals it is a simple, two-step process. Pinch back growth on new plants to keep them compact and to encourage lots of buds. During the growing season, remove fading or dead flower heads so plants look their best and continue to flower. Occasional overall trimming after the first round of blooms is helpful for bushy annuals such as Petunias.

    With perennials, the first action is to pinch back any weak, spindly growth after it emerges in spring. This helps shape plants and encourages lots of strong stems for maximum flower production. Continue to deadhead plants throughout

the growing season while new buds form. Cutting back—removing growth from all over the plant—usually follows flowering and may lead to a second bloom cycle. It keeps plants looking compact and neat and can help revitalize older plants. It also prevents plants from overshadowing neighbors or competing with them for water or nutrients.

Pruning can improve shape

Did You Know?

When you snip off a spent flower, you interrupt the reproduction cycle. A plant's natural response to this is to produce more flowers for more seeds.

Seasonal Tips

SPRING
Pinching
Pinch perennials if the stems look straggly, weak, or leggy. Deadhead and pinch back spring-blooming annuals.

SUMMER
Inspecting
Remove spent flowers, weak or dead stems, and wayward growth. Cut back finished flower stalks to the ground (*above*), unless new buds appear as side shoots. Cut these just above new buds.

FALL
Removing
Remove growth on plants that are in decline, taking off dead shoots at the ground and cutting back others just above new, green growth.

Weather Watch

Early season pinching will result in more blooms later in the season. It will also produce soft, tender, new growth that could be harmed by late frosts. To avoid frost damage, cover plants on cool nights using plastic sheeting or a hot cap and remove during the day.

AFTERCARE

Plants need consistent care, including regular fertilizing and watering after you prune. This gives plants the strength to put out fresh foliage and make new flowers. Applications of a liquid fertilizer at regular intervals will ensure a continual supply of the needed nutrients.

Pinching or cutting back and a boost of fertilizer should result in many new flower stalks, and some will need support. Use bamboo stakes or plastic supports to stake flower stalks before they begin to flop over. This allows maximum flower production.

A Basic Guide to
Dividing Perennials

Enjoy more blooms from your favorite plants when you divide flowering perennials.

DIVIDING PERENNIAL CLUMPS

YOU WILL NEED:

- ❏ Established perennial clump
- ❏ 2 Garden forks
- ❏ Garden knife
- ❏ Pruners
- ❏ Hose

If you are dividing plants with foliage, trim the leaves back by half. With fewer leaves and stems to support, the plant can put its energy underground. Strong root growth and recovery gives plants the best chance for renewed health and better flower production.

1 **In spring,** when new growth appears, soak the ground around the rootball. Dig the perimeter of the rootball using a garden fork.

2 **Lift the clump** and check the condition of the roots. If badly tangled, pry apart large sections using back-to-back forks.

3 **Pull apart healthy** offshoots that have plump, fresh roots and young foliage. Discard any dried up, diseased, or scraggly sections.

4 **Trim broken, bent,** or weak roots and replant in a hole at the same depth as the parent plant. Keep moist and watch for new top growth.

DIVIDING PERENNIALS WITH CROWNS

YOU WILL NEED: ❏ Established perennials with new crowns ❏ Garden fork ❏ Knife

1 **Carefully dig** around the parent plant, keeping the rootball intact. Mix fresh organic material into the soil.

2 **Pull apart** the outermost crowns or use a garden knife to free sections with plump roots and top growth.

3 **Discard the center** of the parent plant if it has died out. Replant the best of the new crown divisions.

Simple Multiplication

Enjoy more flowers and healthier plants by dividing perennials.

Division allows you to maximize flower production

WHY DIVIDE PERENNIALS?

Divide perennials to rejuvenate old plants that have formed crowded masses of stems and roots called clumps. This strengthens original plants for better flower production and gives you new perennials for other areas of the garden. When dividing, separate clumps into sections, or crowns, with foliage and roots that can grow on their own.

Most perennials benefit from division. Those producing smaller and fewer flowers or growing poorly may need dividing. Plants with vigorous new crowns surrounding dead centers should be divided. Divide spreading perennials that crowd neighboring plants to help bring the garden back into control.

HOW TO DIVIDE

Divide perennials according to how they grow. Many, including Daylilies, Asters, and Bleeding-hearts, form large, solid clumps. Divide these by hand if healthy sections pull apart easily. If the mass is entangled, use two garden forks to separate.

For plants that form young crowns around the center, such as Coral Bells and Primroses, dig up and pull off new sections with foliage and roots using your hands or a garden knife. Often the new outer pieces are the healthiest parts of the plant and work best for transplanting. Some perennials, including Irises and Lupines, have very thick, fleshy roots. Divide these by making sharp, clean cuts through the root sections that have smaller feeder roots and foliage attached.

WHEN TO DIVIDE

Divide perennials when your chances for success are highest—during dormancy or well before or after flowering when the weather is mild. This minimizes stress for parent and new plants and helps roots establish.

Divide fall, summer, and late-spring bloomers in spring when they show emerging growth. Choose an overcast day when the soil is moist. In fall, divide plants that have bloomed earlier in the year only if the plants will have some growing time before winter sets in. This allows parent plants to recover and new plants to get established.

Sharp tools make clean cuts

Troubleshooter

It is important for roots to remain moist when dividing. Soak divisions with some soil around roots in a bucket of water, especially if the sections will not be immediately replanted.

A Basic Guide to Dividing Perennials

 ## Seasonal Tips

AFTERCARE

Protect young shoots on newly divided perennials from damage by pests. Slugs and snails may completely destroy foliage on new sections in a night or two. Shiny trails or holes in leaves can indicate their presence. The safest method is to handpick such pests when you see them.

SPRING
Dividing & Fertilizing
Spring is an optimum time to divide most perennials. In late spring after divisions have shown new growth, fertilize by mixing granular fertilizer into soil around each plant *(above)*.

FALL
Dividing
In early fall, divide summer-flowering plants after they finish blooming completely, unless you live in cold regions where plants have no growing time before winter.

WINTER
Protecting
Cover perennials you divided in fall with a layer of mulch. This protective layer will guard against drying winds and cold temperatures.

Weather Watch

The best time to divide perennials is during mild weather in spring and fall. Wait for an overcast morning to dig up clumps and separate new sections. Working under cloudy skies helps roots stay moist and keeps foliage from wilting while you are dividing and replanting your perennials.

One benefit from division is better flower production. Check new growth on parent plants and new transplants a few weeks after division, and stake those that will produce tall flower stalks. Staking early allows you to position wire cages or single stakes without damaging roots or leaves. It also ensures support for the earliest flowers.

A Guide to Rejuvenating a
Perennial Bed

*Bring new life to the garden
when you renew or replace
mature perennials.*

Bringing New Life to Old Gardens

Give your perennial bed special attention to return it to its former splendor and renew its vigor.

WHY REJUVENATE?

Perennials grow for years in the garden but, inevitably, the time comes when they begin to decline and need rejuvenating or replacing. Signs of this stress include poor flower production, dead centers of plants, sprawling growth, or overcrowding. When this happens, you can restore health and increase flower production by dividing, propagating, or replacing the existing plants. Then simply enrich or renew the soil with organic matter and fertilizer to boost fertility and improve drainage.

WHEN TO REJUVENATE?

The best time to work on perennial beds is when plants have just awakened from winter dormancy (early spring) or have slowed down

Rejuvenate beds to give plants enough space to mature

after producing new foliage and flowers. Early spring is best for summer and fall bloomers, while summer or fall, after active periods of growth, is the best time for spring bloomers. This way, plants have maximum recovery time to establish before they bloom the following season.

HOW TO REJUVENATE?

Start by evaluating which plants show signs of decline. Plants with new growth around the perimeter and healthy, but crowded, clumps can be divided (or you can take cuttings to propagate). Discard plants with diseased foliage or no strong growth.

Check the sun and soil needs of any plants that have not grown well. Relocate or

replace any whose requirements do not match the growing conditions in your perennial bed.

Before planting or replanting perennials, at any time of year, be sure to renew the soil by adding organic matter to help plants establish quickly and ensure their health over a long period of time.

Move plants to new locations

Dollar Sense

Dividing crowded, but healthy, perennial plants rejuvenates the original plant and gives you plenty of new divisions for other garden areas. Be sure to plant in favorable conditions.

REJUVENATING A PERENNIAL BED

YOU WILL NEED:

- ❏ Established perennial bed
- ❏ Two garden forks
- ❏ Shovel
- ❏ Organic matter
- ❏ Slow-release fertilizer
- ❏ Rake
- ❏ Fresh perennial plants

1 Evaluate your perennial garden site. Look for any plants showing signs of decline with fewer flowers, dead centers, or overcrowding.

2 Water dry soil. Using a garden fork, loosen soil in the new planting so it mixes easily with compost. Loosen the soil to a depth of 12-18 in.

3 Spread a 2-4 in. layer of compost, manure, or other organic matter and some slow-release fertilizer over the entire planting area.

4 Dig the organic material in deeply, at least 18 in., mixing it well with the native soil. Rake planting area smooth before replanting.

5 For healthy perennials, divide plants to separate new sections and strengthen the original. Use back-to-back garden forks to split clumps.

6 Add plenty of organic matter to planting hole. Replant new sections or new perennials in the garden. Allow at least 12 in. between plants.

Seasonal Tips

SPRING
Dividing & Planting
Dig and divide when new growth emerges and soil can be worked (*above*). This is also a good time to add new perennials to the garden.

SUMMER
Propagating
After they bloom, divide or take cuttings from spring-flowering perennials to restore existing plants and generate new sections to increase your plantings.

EARLY FALL
Rejuvenating
If you live where plants will have some growing time before winter, rejuvenate beds now. This allows plants to establish for spring.

Weather Watch

Your newly planted perennial divisions or nursery-bought plants may suffer damage from hot sun during heat waves. Construct a newspaper tent or use a pre-formed paper hotcap to cover your plants during afternoon heat. Keep plants well watered.

AFTERCARE

Soil moisture is the most critical element for plants putting out new roots. Thoroughly water newly divided or planted perennials at planting time and check periodically to determine soil moisture level. Water as needed, but avoid soggy soil.

Apply a generous layer of mulch to help retain soil moisture, discourage weeds, and give the garden a finished look. Add a ring of mulch around plants, starting 1-2 in. from the base of each plant.

Be sure to add extra fertilizer to beds the growing season following rejuvenation. Apply just before the main growth cycle and flowering period of the perennials start.

PLANT GUIDE

Coreopsis

Warm yellow blossoms to brighten sunny gardens

Season	Special Features	Best Conditions	
Annual or perennial	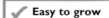 Easy to grow	Zones 3-10	
Flowers from summer to frost	Self-seeding	Full sun	Height: 1-3 ft.
	Fast growing	Average, well-drained soil	Spread: 2-3 ft.

Mounds of Cheery Gold

Free-blooming and sun-loving, Coreopsis offers bright bouquets for garden color and cutting.

COLORS & VARIETIES

Covered with long-stemmed blossoms, Coreopsis grow in low, rambling, bushy mounds of bright green, soft foliage. Their carefree nature makes them choice candidates for the leisure gardener.

Most varieties bloom in shades of golden yellow, but a few, such as 'Brown Eyes', have darker maroon centers. Some cultivars, such as the 18-20 in., double 'Sunray', have a more compact form and are less prone to sprawl.

Plant Threadleaf Coreopsis for the easiest of mid-summer perennial blooms. 'Golden Showers' is a spritely, golden yellow, drought-resistant plant with deep green, feathery leaves and many branching stems.

Annual *Coreopsis tinctoria* grows rapidly to nearly 3 ft. and is able to thrive even in poor, dry soils. *C. maritima,* an excellent annual cutting flower, may overwinter in warmer areas.

'Moonbeam' over a stone wall

Soft pink C. rosea

WHERE TO PLANT

Coreopsis deserves a prominent place in your landscape in informal flower beds, on sunny slopes, or in naturalized meadow gardens where they have ample room to spread.

Group three or more 'Baby Sun' Coreopsis in an out-of-the-way corner for a nearly maintenance-free, good-looking spot of color.

Use Coreopsis' free-flowing blooms to hide unsightly areas. A mound planted between evergreens in a foundation planting will mask any gaps and provide a dash of color. The same plants can also be used to conceal the fading leaves of spring bulbs.

On a patio, fill a brick planter so that it overflows with Coreopsis. The yellow blooms contrast nicely against the red-brown of the brick and the plant appreciates the reflected heat from the patio.

'Zagreb' Threadleaf Coreopsis

Radiant 'Baby Sun'

PERFECT PARTNERS

The pleasingly bright colors of Coreopsis combine well with other plants in the summer landscape. Placed at intervals or meandering through other perennials and shrubs, they provide bright, visual accents.

...lows in a perennial bed

Contrast strong summer blues of Veronicas and Salvias with compact 'Sunburst'. The Coreopsis' gold blooms last into fall when they accent the yellow centers of purple Asters.

Feature the fine texture and pale yellow blossoms of feathery 'Moonbeam' among Nicotianas and tall, white Snapdragons in a container. Or, highlight its delicacy with the lilac-pink spikes of Gayfeathers and clumps of Blue Oat Grass.

Weave tumbling masses of long-blooming 'Goldfink' through the rich, deep red-and-orange hues of 'Lucifer' and orange-yellow 'Solfatare' Crocosmias. Back the scene with bicolored Gloriosa ~sies for a dazzling display.

PLANTING & AFTERCARE

YOU WILL NEED: ❑ Coreopsis seeds ❑ Shovel ❑ Rake ❑ Compost ❑ Hose with fine spray nozzle

1 In early spring, loosen the top 6-8 in. of garden soil with a shovel. Mix in a 2-4 in. layer of compost; use more for heavier soils.

2 Rake ground to break up clumps and remove stones. Scatter seeds lightly over area. Do not cover, as seeds require light to sprout.

3 Moisten ground with a fine spray. Water regularly until plants reach 6 in. tall. Thin to 12 in. apart and decrease watering.

4 Water infrequently, only to keep soil from drying out completely. Cut off faded flowers to promote summer-long blooming.

Tip

The seedlings created from your Coreopsis plants through self-sowing may differ in appearance from the named cultivars you planted. To get more of a particular variety of plant, divide the mature plants. Deadhead faded Coreopsis flowers often to prevent unwanted seedlings.

Secrets of Success

BUYING HINTS

SUN & SOIL

SPECIAL ADVICE

- **Buy seeds** from garden centers or nursery catalogs in late winter. Look for healthy, potted plants in nurseries in the spring.
- **Avoid purchasing** plants with dark spots or yellow bumps on leaves, as these may have a fungal disease.

- **Full sun.** Coreopsis will tolerate a little shade only in the early morning or very late afternoon.
- **Well-drained soil.** Coreopsis bloom prolifically in average, even poor, dry soil, but they do not thrive in excessively moist soil.

- **Transplant seedlings** or divide plants every two to four years to preserve Coreopsis in your garden.
- **Coreopsis thrive** beside walks and walls where they get reflected heat. They can withstand heat and dry soil better than most flowers.

 Seasonal Tips

LATE WINTER
Sowing
Sow Coreopsis seeds indoors eight weeks before last frost in pots or flats filled with sterile potting mix. Keep the pots warm, 70-75 degrees F., until seeds sprout. Seeds will germinate in two to three weeks.

SPRING
Planting & Dividing
Set out seedlings and new plants after all danger of frost is past. Divide older plants every three years to maintain vigorous growth.

SUMMER
Maintaining
Remove unsightly faded brown blossoms regularly. Or, shear entire plant when flowering has slowed down *(below)*. This stimulates renewed growth as well as a repeat flush of blooms.

 Plant Doctor

The spotted Cucumber beetle sometimes eats small holes in Coreopsis foliage. It rarely causes severe damage, and it does not usually affect the plants' growth. When you see the beetles on leaves, handpick and put in a jar of soapy water and let sit overnight.

Delphiniums

Majestic flowering spires for the summer border

Season	Special Features	Best Conditions	
P Annual or perennial ✳ Flowers in summer	✂ Good for cutting 🐦 Attractive to wildlife	🌐 Zones 3-11 ▦ Full sun to partial shade 🔧 Rich, well-drained soil	

The Artistocrat of Perennials

Dramatic Delphiniums offer pastel towers of elegant blooms to the garden.

COLORS & VARIETIES

Delphiniums are prized for their intense blue flowers, though they also come in violet, pink, or white shades. Many have a charming "bee" or central cluster of petals in a contrasting color, and all carry deeply cut, green foliage below their blooms.

The statuesque 'Pacific Giant Series' grows 5 ft. or more and must be staked. Staking is not necessary for the 2 ½ ft. 'Magic Fountains' hybrids or the bushier 'Connecticut Yankee' strain. All three strains are available in the full range of vibrant Delphinium shades.

The 3-4 ft. 'Belladonna' hybrids are less upright than other varieties, producing many branching stems and white or blue blooms most of the summer.

The neon blue 'Blue Bird'

Spires of white 'Galahad'

WHERE TO PLANT

Towering Delphiniums are classic components of perennial borders and cottage gardens alike. The shorter varieties are perfect for growing in containers.

Plant drifts of tall Delphiniums that bloom in the same color, such as the azure 'Blue Bird' with its white bee or the all-white 'Galahad', at the back of a border behind other plants.

Shorter Delphiniums bring color and substance to the middle of the border and are also ideal for lining walkways. A mix of violet, rose, cream, and blue spikes will accentuate a winding garden path.

The smaller varieties are decorative in containers for the terrace or near the front door. Try edging the pots with white Sweet Alyssum or trailing Lobelia for a simple, yet graceful, effect.

Drifts of tall Delphiniums add

PERFECT PARTNERS

The intense colors of traditional blue Delphiniums contrast beautifully with soft pastels and clear whites of other perennials. Choose companions with grass-like leaves or rounded forms for additional interest.

Pair the tall, deep violet 'Black Knight' with mauve Columbines and chartreuse Lady's-mantle for a stunning contrast. 'Summer Skies' has sky blue flowers with a whit bee and creates a wonderful pastel partnership with the pink blooms of Lavatera.

Pale yellow 'Sunglean and deep lavender 'Might Atom' Delphiniums blend beautifully with white Sha.

...legance to a formal hedge

Daisies and silver Artemesias. Ignite this planting with fiery orange Oriental Poppies.

...ing Arthur' with Lavatera

PLANTING & AFTERCARE

YOU WILL NEED: ❏ Delphinium seedlings ❏ Compost ❏ Spading fork ❏ Trowel ❏ Bone meal

1 **As soon as the soil** can be worked in spring, prepare a 2 ft. square for each seedling. Fork in 2-4 in. of well-rotted compost.

2 **With a trowel,** make holes 6 in. deep and 2 ft. apart. Work a small handful of bone meal into the bottom of each hole.

3 **Plant the seedlings,** taking care not to cover the root crown (where the stems and roots meet) with soil. Water to settle plants.

4 **After flowers fade,** cut spikes below the lowest flower. When new shoots are 6 in. tall, cut old stalks completely to ground.

◇ *Tip* ◇

For tall-growing varieties, set sturdy stakes as soon as the stalks begin to grow. Be careful not to damage the roots. The stakes should be two-thirds the expected height of the flowering stalks. As the stalks grow, tie them loosely to the stakes at 1 ft. intervals with soft twine or yarn.

69

Secrets of Success

BUYING HINTS

- **Buy seedlings** in 4 in. pots, choosing young plants with healthy leaves. Plant in early spring for the most abundant flowers.
- **Avoid overgrown** plants that have already begun to form flower stalks, as these will not bloom as heavily.

SUN & SOIL

- **Full sun or partial** shade. In cool-summer climates, plant in full sun; where summers are hot, plant in dappled shade.
- **Rich, well-drained soil.** Add plenty of compost before planting and water well during dry spells.

SPECIAL ADVICE

- **In areas with hot** summers and mild winters, treat Delphiniums as annuals. In colder climates, they can thrive for many years as perennials.
- **Plant Delphiniums** near fences, walls, or hedges to protect them from wind.

 ## Seasonal Tips

LATE WINTER
Ordering seeds
Look to mail-order companies for seed mixes and single-color varieties.

EARLY SPRING
Sowing
Start seeds indoors in fine potting soil in flats eight to ten weeks before planting. Move seedlings to individual pots when they have two sets of true leaves.

LATE SPRING
Planting
Transplant seedlings into the garden only after all danger of frost has passed.

LATE FALL
Cleaning up
After the first hard frost, cut back stems and foliage *(below)* to prevent diseases and discourage insects.

 ## Plant Doctor

Snails and slugs can devour young plants. Spread horticultural diatomaceous earth, available at most garden centers, around Delphiniums to deter these pests. The silica-rich earth will pierce the pests' skin and kill them.

Gloriosa Daisies

Tall, brilliant sunbursts of summer color

Season	Special Features	Best Conditions	
Perennial	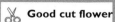 Good cut flower	Zones 4-8	
Flowers all summer	Self-seeding	Full sun	
	Easy care	Ordinary soil	

A Stunning Wildflower

Gloriosa Daisies are the perfect choice for tough plants that will provide color all summer.

COLORS & VARIETIES

Gloriosa Daisies are cultivars of a classic summer flower, the Black-eyed Susan (*Rudbeckia hirta*). Although they are perennials, they cannot survive cold winters and are usually grown as annuals except in warmer areas of the country. These flowers will usually drop seeds, producing new flowers the next spring.

The spectacular flowers of the Gloriosa Daisy grow up to 6 in. wide on plants that often reach 3 ft. tall. The flowers bloom in orange, yellow, mahogany, russet, and deeper reds. Gloriosa Double Daisy carries smaller-than-average flowers, but with a double row of petals.

Choose 'Green Eyes' for a truly unusual flower to include in your garden. This Gloriosa Daisy features deep yellow petals surrounding simple, light green centers.

Gloriosa Daisies in a pot

The unique 'Green Eyes'

WHERE TO PLANT

Gloriosa Daisies are ideal for an informal border or a bed along a wood fence. They are also some of the best flowers for a cut-flower garden.

Fill a wooden barrel with the sunny shades of 'Pinwheel'. This variety offers bright blooms with bands of mahogany and gold.

Edge the front of an annual flower border with 'Goldilocks', offering open, 3-4 in. blooms on 8-10 in. stems. It is named for its brilliant, gold petals.

Line the back of flower bed with a mix of Gloriosa Daisy cultivars. Their bushy growth and large blooms will fill the bed with sunny color.

PERFECT PARTNERS

The stiff, upright form of these large-flowered plants makes them good for pairing with other tall plants.

Ornamental grasses are sensational with Gloriosa

'Rustic Colors' with pink Peon[...]

Daisies. Combine Variegated Maiden Grass (*Miscanthus sinensis* 'Variegatus') with drifts of 'Marmalade'. This Gloriosa Daisy grows 2 ft. tal[l] with yellow-orange blooms.

Providing lush blooms late in the summer, the rusty pink hues of Sedum 'Autumn Joy' will keep 'Rustic Colors' company while other summer flowers go to seed.

Create a stunning bed by planting generous patches of bronze, 2 ft. 'Rustic Dwarfs' with Zinnias. The bed will provide a riot of color in the garden and endless vases of cut flowers all season long.

A [...]

...es, purple Mullein and Yarrow

...vibrant Gloriosa Daisy bloom

PLANTING & AFTERCARE

YOU WILL NEED: ❑ Gloriosa Daisy seeds
❑ Hoe ❑ Rake ❑ Weed-free straw

1 **Using a hoe,** dig up the bed that will be seeded to a depth of 8 in. Remove all large stones and weeds as you prepare the area.

2 **Break up any clumps** of soil you encounter and level area with a rake. Draw rake across the bed, leaving ½ in. deep furrows.

3 **Sprinkle the seeds** into these furrows, spacing them 2-3 in. apart. Lightly cover seeds with a thin layer of soil.

4 **Firm the bed** slightly with the back of the rake. Cover with a ½ in. layer of weed-free straw and water with a fine mist.

5 **Once seedlings** appear, thin to 6 in. between plants. As they mature, thin to 1 ft. apart by moving extra seedlings to another site.

Tip

Cut off the mature blooms of your Gloriosa Daisies regularly to keep these plants strong and blooming well into fall.

Gloriosa Daisies

Secrets of Success

BUYING HINTS

- **Buy seeds** in early spring. If you are planting late in the season, look for sturdy seedlings; the bigger they are, the better.
- **Avoid seedlings** with soft, mushy leaves. They have been overwatered and may die after transplanting.

SUN & SOIL

- **Full sun.** A Gloriosa Daisy needs strong, direct sun to grow upright and stiff. Six hours each day is the minimum requirement.
- **Average, well-drained** soil. Ordinary soil will suffice. In hot areas, mulch to keep the roots cool.

SPECIAL ADVICE

- **Shake water** off their wide, flat flowers after it rains. The extra weight can bend the Gloriosa Daisy.
- **In cold winter areas,** mulch heavily around the roots of plants and they may survive to bloom the following summer.

 Seasonal Tips

SPRING
Planting
After the soil warms, plant seeds. Cover with a layer of mulch if the weather is cold.

SUMMER
Maintaining
Stake top-heavy flowers *(right)*. Water deeply and mulch with compost or straw as the weather heats up.

FALL
Self-seeding
Help your plants self-seed by leaving some of the flowers on the plant so that the seedpods can mature. In late fall, cut the plants back to 6 in. stumps, but leave the spent flowers and stems on the ground so that the seeds can easily germinate later.

 Plant Doctor

Leaf miners can damage Gloriosa Daisies. These are larvae that burrow between leaf layers, leaving squiggly tunnels and brown blotches. Use floating row cover in early summer to keep adults from laying their eggs on plants, or spray with an appropriate insecticide.

Heleniums

Glowing flowers to enhance the late summer garden

Season	Special Features	Best Conditions	
P Perennial	✓ Easy to grow	🌐 Zones 3-11	
❋ Flowers in late summer or fall	✂ Good for cutting	☀ Full sun	Height: 2 ½-5 ft.
	🕷 Disease resistant	⛏ Moist, well-drained soil	◄─Spread: 1 ½-2 ½ ft.

Tawny Tints of Autumn

Heleniums provide a brilliant tapestry of color on tall, sturdy plants.

COLORS & VARIETIES

Heleniums bloom profusely from late summer through fall on spreading, branching plants to 5 ft. tall, offering valuable color to the garden after many other flowers are past their peak.

The 2-3 in. wide flowers are available in rich shades of yellow, orange, red, or burgundy, each centered with a prominent, velvety yellow or brown cone. Though commonly referred to as "Sneezeweed", Heleniums do not actually cause people to sneeze.

At 30 in. tall and 20 in. wide, 'Wyndley' is one of the most compact Heleniums. It bears orange-yellow flowers for an exceptionally long period of time.

A particularly popular variety, 'Moerheim Beauty' produces rich mahogany-colored flowers that fade to burnt orange on a 3 ft. plant. 'Riverton Beauty' grows to

Helenium 'Sunshine'

5 ft. tall and has yellow flowers with purplish brown central cones.

WHERE TO PLANT

Heleniums grow and bloom best when planted in a location that receives lots of sun. Give each plant a couple of square feet so the roots can spread and plants will not compete for nutrients.

Plant Heleniums on the sunny side of a hedge or simple fence. An uncluttered background will keep the spotlight on the Heleniums' colorful blossoms.

Heleniums are a wonderful addition to the back of a large, informal border, where their unstructured appearance and late-season bloom can be fully appreciated.

Able to tolerate damp (though not soggy) soil better than many other perennials, Heleniums are a good choice for planting near a garden pond.

Heleniums with Chrysanthemu

PERFECT PARTNERS

For maximum impact in the late summer and fall garden, combine Heleniums with other tall, late-blooming perennials and annuals.

Plant Helenium 'Brilliant', which has deep chestnut-colored flowers, with the rusty pink blooms of Sedum 'Autumn Joy'. For a striking contrast, add tall, white-flowered Boltonia 'Snowbank' to the planting.

The golden yellow blossoms of 'Butterpat' Heleniums make a cheerful late-season picture when combined with soothing cornflower blue Asters.

'Bruno', a 4 ft. Helenium with deep bronze-red flowers

'Wyndley' with Agapanthus

as and Rose Campions

and dark green foliage, is an outstanding complement to the neutral colors and the different textures of many ornamental grasses, such as Feather Reed Grass or Giant Feather Grass.

The gold-bronze 'Cymbal Star'

PLANTING & AFTERCARE

YOU WILL NEED: ❏ Heleniums in containers ❏ Spading fork or shovel ❏ Compost ❏ Bucket of water

1 **In spring, prepare** the soil for planting. Remove weeds and loosen the soil to a depth of 8 in. Dig in a 2 in. layer of compost.

2 **Remove plants** from containers. Soak in a bucket of water for 30 minutes to restore moisture and loosen the roots.

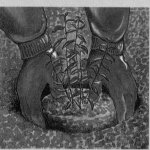

3 **Dig a hole** the depth of the rootball for each plant. Set the plant into the soil at the same depth it grew in the container.

4 **Gently firm soil** around the roots with hands. Water well to ensure good contact between the roots and soil.

5 **Heleniums need** regular watering. Apply at least an inch of water a week during dry spells, using a soaker hose or sprinkler.

Tip

Established Helenium plants should be divided regularly in the spring or fall. Dig up entire plant, divide, and replant or discard extras.

Secrets of Success

BUYING HINTS

- **Buy Helenium plants** in early spring. Look for healthy, even foliage and new buds and shoots emerging from the base.
- **Avoid leggy or wilted** Heleniums and any that have roots protruding from the drainage holes.

SUN & SOIL

- **Full sun.** Heleniums need sun all day to flower well. Do not plant Heleniums where they will be shaded by trees or structures.
- **Moist, well-drained** soil. Add extra compost to sandy soil to help hold moisture around the roots.

SPECIAL ADVICE

- **To encourage** sturdier growth and prevent plants from becoming straggly, pinch back the growing tip of each stem in spring.
- **To help prevent** soil from drying, spread compost around the plants. Renew the mulch each spring.

 ## Seasonal Tips

EARLY SPRING
Planting
Sow or plant Heleniums early in spring after danger of frost has passed.

LATE SPRING
Pinching
To increase flowering and bushiness, pinch 1-2 in. off shoots when plants are one-third their ultimate height.

SUMMER
Staking
Taller varieties of Heleniums usually require staking before they become heavy with flowers. Place stake around plant and loop with twine.

FALL
Deadheading
To keep Helenium plants blooming through the fall season, regularly cut off any spent flowers *(below)*.

 ## Plant Doctor

Heleniums are fairly disease and pest resistant. Snails do, however, attack foliage, chewing leaf edges at night. Handpicking is effective for small problems but larger ones may require the use of snail baits purchased from nurseries.

Lamb's-ears
Soft and shimmery leaves of silver

Season	Special Features	Best Conditions	
Perennial	Good groundcover	Zones 4-11	
Flowers in summer	Fast growing	Full sun	Height: 6-18 in.
	Drought resistant	Well-drained soil	Spread: 18-24 in.

Rich, Velvety Texture

The broad, woolly foliage of Lamb's-ears makes a striking foil for other plants.

COLORS & VARIETIES

Lamb's-ears *(Stachys byzantia)* grows quickly into a dense mat of 3-6 in. long, silvery leaves covered with short, soft hairs, giving them the look and feel of a baby lamb's ear. Some varieties produce 2 ft. flower stalks with whorls of small, mauve-pink flowers.

'Cotton Boll' is a compact cultivar with flowers that are only partially developed, resembling little, woolly cotton balls.

'Silver Carpet' seldom forms flowers at all, instead making a thick, low, rapidly spreading carpet of downy, silvery-hued foliage. The mat-forming 'Rosca' bears tubular, clear pink flowers in summer above deep green, oval leaves that are visible until frost.

'Big Ears', also known as 'Helene von Stein', bears long leaves reaching up to 6 in. or more in length. Its flowers are insignificant.

Stachys byzantia by a path

Broad-leaved 'Wave Hill'

WHERE TO PLANT

Lamb's-ears easily fill a variety of roles in the garden, serving as edging plants for borders or along pathways, as an attractive rock garden accent, or as a groundcover.

Plant Lamb's-ears as an edging in front of a flower border, where it will provide a sense of continuity, or to spill over and soften the edges of a stone, brick, or concrete path or driveway.

Take advantage of the fast-spreading nature of 'Silver Carpet' Lamb's-ears by planting it as an easy-to-grow groundcover under shrubs.

Simulate a dry stream bed with a mass planting of Lamb's-ears positioned to "flow" in between and around the boulders in a large rock garden.

PERFECT PARTNERS

The silvery gray leaves and soft, low profile of Lamb's-ears provide a flattering and

Lamb's-ears planted with Petun

Fuzzy 'Cotton Boll'

effective contrast to many other plants.

Red and gold flowers seem to sparkle when paired with the gray foliage of any Lamb's-ears. Try planting bright Scarlet Sage and Penstemon 'Garnet' or clear yellow Evening Primrose and

...as, Daisies, and a Rose

Corn Marigold near Lamb's-ears for an eye-catching and delightful combination.

'Primrose Heron', a Lamb's-ears with chartreuse foliage in spring, fading to gray-green in summer, looks great planted with Golden Oregano and 'Crater Lake Blue' Veronica.

The large leaves of 'Big Ears' make a subtle but interesting contrast planted with other gray-leaved plants. Pair 'Big Ears' with the soft gray leaves and purple-blue blooms of Catmint, Russian Sage, and Lavender Cotton to create a subtle woodland edging or to soften and hide the bottom edge of a sunny, wooden deck.

PLANTING & AFTERCARE

YOU WILL NEED: ❑ Flat of Lamb's-ears plants ❑ Spading fork ❑ Rake ❑ Compost

1 **Plant Lamb's-ears** as a groundcover in spring or fall. Use a spading fork to loosen the soil to a depth of at least 8 in.

2 **Work in 2 in.** of compost and rake smooth. Slide plants out of flat. Separate into smaller clumps with your fingers.

3 **Dig holes big enough** for roots, spacing them 12 in. apart. Place plants in holes, spreading out roots. Firm soil around each plant.

4 **Water the area with** a hose, to thoroughly moisten root area and settle the soil. Water again when the surface of the soil dries.

Dollar Sense

To fill in bare spots or plant a new area, divide Lamb's-ears in spring or fall. With a shovel, dig up rooted sections or clumps from the edges of an existing patch. Pull them apart into small plants. Replant in soil amended with compost. Water immediately after planting.

81

Secrets of Success

BUYING HINTS

- **Buy Lamb's-ears** in flats or 4 in. or 1 gal. containers. Choose plants with firm, healthy foliage.
- **Avoid plants** with limp-looking or mushy-feeling leaves. Do not buy flats of Lamb's-ears with any bare spots between plants.

SUN & SOIL

- **Full sun.** In most climates, Lamb's-ears grow best in full sun, but they do appreciate some afternoon shade in very hot areas.
- **Well-drained soil.** Although Lamb's-ears will tolerate poor soils, adding compost improves growth.

SPECIAL ADVICE

- **Plant Lamb's-ears** along paths where the luminous leaves reflect artificial light or moonlight and lead evening garden strollers.
- **In hot, humid** climates, water Lamb's-ears early in the day (so leaves dry before night) to prevent rotting.

 ## Seasonal Tips

 ## Plant Doctor

LATE WINTER
Starting seeds
Although varieties of Lamb's-ears that form few flowering stems must be propagated by division, the common Lamb's-ears is easy to grow from seed. Sow seeds in flats indoors, keeping the temperature at 70 degrees F. Set seedlings in the garden in late spring or early fall.

EARLY SPRING
Trimming
After last frost, trim off dead leaves from plants. New growth will soon appear.

SUMMER
Cutting back
Remove spent stems after the flowers fade (below). Some gardeners prefer to remove stems as they appear, growing Lamb's-ears for the foliage effect alone.

In humid climates, Lamb's-ears is subject to "melt out"—leaf diseases caused by fungi. The affected foliage quickly rots and dies. Remove any dead leaves by hand or with a rake. New growth will appear once the weather has cooled.

Lavateras

An extravaganza of fabulous, fluted blooms

Season	Special Features	Best Conditions	
P Annual and perennial	✢ Self-seeds freely	⊕ All zones	
✱ Flowers in summer and fall	✦ Fast growing	☀ Full sun to partial shade	Height: 2-6 ft.
✿ Repeat blooms	✂ Good for cutting	🔨 Average, well-drained soil	← Spread: 2-6 ft.

Brilliant, Silken Colors

Glorious Lavateras provide a profusion of showstopping, mauve blooms with little care.

COLORS & VARIETIES

Lavateras are fast-growing summer bloomers that are often referred to as Mallows. Their wide, rosy purple or white blossoms densely cover the upright, shrubby plants. The solitary blooms of Lavateras are reminiscent of glossy Hollyhocks.

Compact, annual forms of Rose Mallow (*Lavatera trimestris)* quickly become branching, soft-stemmed mounds of lobed, dark green leaves densely covered with showstopping blooms. 'Mont Rose' is a 2-3 ft. favorite with rose pink petals; 'Mont Blanc' is similar with cream-colored centers on white blossoms.

Often grown as an annual, *L. thuringiaca* assumes a larger presence in the garden, growing as tall as 6 ft. In mild, coastal regions, it remains a nearly ever-blooming perennial. The tall, distinctive cultivar 'Barnsley' opens nearly white and matures to a pale pink with a darker center.

WHERE TO PLANT

Plant Lavateras where you want a bright splash of color or to mask an unsightly background. Their exuberant masses can fill a dull, empty corner or an open expanse along a roadside.

Lavateras' tall, imposing forms provide easy color against an unsightly building or fence. The abundant, summer-long blooms can cover an exposed wall or create a temporary screen.

Create a focal point in an island bed with tall, less open varieties. Try sturdy 'Kew Rose' for its contrast of gray-green, felted foliage and brilliant pink blossoms.

Tall and short varieties are especially useful when planted in groups for a quick, single-year hedge. Plant a line of bushy, 3-4 ft. varieties such as rose 'Loveliness' along a path or driveway.

Rose Mallow 'Silver Cup'

'Mont Blanc' in a flower bed

Lovely 'Pink Frills' hovers abo

PERFECT PARTNERS

Lavateras' intense colors create stunning effects when planted among flowers in paler tones.

Blend compact forms, such as bright pink 'Silver Cup' or the more delicate 'Pink Beauty', into a border between 'Pink Mist' Scabious and white 'Omega' Phlox.

Build up a sequence of warm colors with the varied pink hues of 'Indian Carpet' Sweet Williams, spires of magenta Snapdragons, and the 6 ft. tall mounds of 'Pink Frills' Lavateras.

Accent rose pink, 5 ft. tall 'Rosea' with the soft, silver-gray foliage of 'Powis Castle' Artemisias and 'Silve

'Hidcote' Lavenders

Carpet' Lamb's-ears. The tiers of color will intermingle nicely, but the showy rose color of the large, Hibiscus-like Lavatera flowers will stand out against the low, silvery background.

Unusual Lavatera 'Variegata'

PLANTING & AFTERCARE

YOU WILL NEED: ❏ Lavatera seeds ❏ 3 in. pots ❏ Germinating mix ❏ Plastic wrap ❏ Trowel ❏ Compost

1 Six weeks before the last frost date, fill 3 in. pots with a pre-moistened germinating mix. Plant seeds 1/4 in. deep and water lightly.

2 Cover pots loosely with plastic wrap to keep moist. Place in a warm spot. Remove the plastic wrap after seeds sprout.

3 When plants are about four weeks old, harden off by setting out a few hours each day for a week before planting outside.

4 When frost danger has passed, dig holes slightly larger than pot, about 2 ft. apart. Mix a trowelful of compost into each hole.

5 Set plants in holes. Fill in with soil, firming well, and water. Cut flowers regularly and deadhead to encourage constant blooms.

Tip

Cut back long branches of faded flower stalks to a lower leaf to keep your Lavateras compact and blooming all summer.

Secrets of Success

BUYING HINTS

SUN & SOIL

SPECIAL ADVICE

● **Buy seeds for named** varieties from seed catalogs in late winter. Look for plants in spring at nurseries and garden centers.
● **Avoid Lavateras with** rust marks on leaves. Do not buy yellowed or spindly, unbranched plants.

● **Full sun.** Lavateras can tolerate heat and do best in full sun. They will also do well in partial shade but not in high humidity.
● **Well-drained, average** soil. For a long season of blooms, amend soil with slow-release fertilizer.

● **For continuous blooms,** sow annual Lavateras at intervals throughout the spring until nighttime temperatures remain above 50 degrees F.
● **Pinch back** the top stems of Lavateras to encourage bushier, branching growth.

 ## Seasonal Tips

 ## Plant Doctor

EARLY SPRING
Sowing
Sow seeds indoors six weeks prior to your last frost date. Sow seeds outdoors where plants will grow after all danger of frost is past.

SUMMER
Maintaining
Cut flowering branches regularly for constant summer blooms *(right)*. Remove stems from the sides to encourage added plant height. To propagate Lavateras, take plant cuttings at the start of summer.

FALL
Cleaning up
Collect seeds from ripe seedpods for sowing next spring. After your first frost, or when plants have stopped blooming, cut stems to the ground, chop, and add to your compost pile.

Lavateras can be affected by scale insects that attach to leaves and stems and damage the plant by sucking its juices. Prune out and destroy any heavily infested branches. Spray plants with a lightweight horticultural oil ("summer oil") to control scale.

Lupines

Dense flower spikes tower above striking foliage

Season	Special Features	Best Conditions	
Annual or perennial	**Good for cutting**	**All zones**	
Flowers in spring or early summer	**Some varieties: fragrant**	**Full sun to partial shade**	
	Self-seeding	**Well-drained soil**	

Height: 1-5 ft.

Spread: 1-2 ft.

Vivid Columns of Color

Lupines provide brilliant flowers and a valuable vertical accent in the early summer garden.

COLORS & VARIETIES

Striking Lupines grow tall spikes of Sweet Pea-shaped flowers in blue, white, pink, cream, yellow, orange, red, or purple, as well as striking bicolors, in early summer above attractive clumps of divided foliage.

The most widely grown Lupines are the 2-3 ft., perennial 'Russell Hybrids', refined versions of the taller Washington Lupine. Several shorter perennial Lupines have been bred from these

hybrids, such as 18 in. 'Little Lulu'. All are available in the full range of Lupine colors.

Other garden Lupines are annual wildflowers that will grow in all zones, such as the 1 ft., blue-and-white or pink, spring-blooming Texas Bluebonnets. Sky Lupine is a 1-2 ft., fragrant, easy-to-grow West Coast native with rich blue flowers marked with white in spring. Other annual Lupines include the 2-3 ft., blue-and-pink *Lupinus hartwegi* and fragrant, 2 ft. Yellow Lupine.

WHERE TO PLANT

With their showy flowers and good-looking foliage, Lupines are a delightful addition to borders, cottage gardens, and wildflower meadows.

Plant dwarf hybrids, such as the 20 in. 'Gallery Series', available in the full range of popular Lupine colors, near the front of a border. These look best in groups of five or more.

Maroon Lupines tower above cl

For a simple, handsome display, place a drift of the tall, pink-and-white perennial 'The Chatelaine' Lupines in front of a hedge or fence.

Plant the wildflower Lupines along with masses of other wildflowers to create a colorful, natural meadow.

PERFECT PARTNERS

The wide range of plant sizes and flower colors yield many possibilities for using Lupines in effective combinations.

Perennial Lupines, such as the 18-24 in. 'Popsicle' mixture, are charming in a cottage garden with Peonies, Delphiniums, and Pinks.

Combine the white- flowered 'Gallery Series' selection with red Oriental

Blue 'Russell Hybrids'

Pink 'Russell Hybrids' edging a natural wood fence

eery Helianthus

Poppies for a wonderful contrast of color and form.

The blue-and-white form of 'Band of Nobles' hybrid Lupine complements tall, white Bearded Irises perfectly. Edge the bed with mixed 'Easter Bonnet' Sweet Alyssum for a soft effect.

Lupines with Dianthus

PLANTING & AFTERCARE

YOU WILL NEED: ❏ Lupine seeds ❏ Knife or nail file ❏ Packaged potting soil ❏ Peat pots

1 **In late winter,** scarify, or nick, Lupine seeds with a knife or nail file and sow in peat pots filled with dampened potting soil.

2 **Sow two seeds** in each peat pot. Cover the seeds with a ¼ in. layer of potting soil. Water gently with a spray bottle.

3 **Keep pots** indoors in a cool (68 degrees F. or less) spot. Seeds should germinate in three weeks. Water when surface is dry.

4 **Thin to one** plant per pot when seedlings are 1 in. tall. As planting time nears, set outside for a few hours a day to harden off.

5 **Transplant Lupines** into the garden after frost has passed. Tear off pot rim to prevent water loss. Plant whole pot in bed.

Tip

After blooming, cut back perennial Lupines to help prevent self-seeding, which weakens plants. Let annual types self-sow.

Secrets of Success

BUYING HINTS

- **Buy Lupine plants** in spring in 4 in. or 1 gal. pots, choosing those with strong, healthy top growth. Or, purchase seeds in spring.
- **Avoid Lupine plants** with weak top growth and either underdeveloped or crowded roots.

SUN & SOIL

- **Full sun to partial shade.** Lupines grow best in areas with cool summers. They will not bloom well in areas with high humidity.
- **Well-drained, slightly** acidic soil. Work in plenty of compost before planting, but do not add lime.

SPECIAL ADVICE

- **Stake tall Lupines** when they are young to prevent breakage. Use bamboo stakes and soft twine.
- **Annual Lupines can be** sown outdoors after last frost; sow perennial seeds in early spring, or in early autumn in mild-winter areas.

 ## Seasonal Tips

SPRING
Planting & Fertilizing
Pull back any mulch that was applied before the previous winter. Plant Lupine seedlings after last frost. Feed Lupines with a slow-release fertilizer each spring, following the directions on the label.

SUMMER
Watering
Water Lupines deeply during dry periods. A thick mulch of shredded leaves or straw will help to keep the soil moist and cool.

LATE FALL
Mulching
After the first frosts of fall, add another layer of mulch, such as wood chips or shredded leaves, to protect and insulate the plants over the winter *(below)*.

 ## Plant Doctor

Lupines are sometimes affected by unsightly powdery mildew. The mildew may cause gray or white powdery patches to appear on the plant's stems and leaves. Pick off diseased leaves and destroy badly infected plants. Plant Lupines in well-ventilated areas to prevent mildew.

New England Asters

A feast of flowers that glow with color through fall

Season	Special Features	Best Conditions	
Perennial Flowers in late summer and fall	Easy to grow Fast growing Good for cutting Self-seeding	Zones 4-8 Full sun to partial shade Average soil	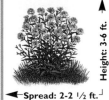 Height: 3-6 ft. Spread: 2-2 ½ ft.

Late Season Classics

Long-blooming New England Asters enhance the fall garden for many weeks.

COLORS & VARIETIES

New England Asters are similar to New York Asters but grow taller, with thicker stems, and have rough, hairy leaves to 5 in. long. Their flowers have many petals, giving them a frilly look. Wild varieties of New England Asters have deep purple blossoms, while named varieties flower in white and various shades of pink, lilac, and purple.

'Harrington Pink' New England Aster has clear, silvery pink flowers with yellow centers that shine on 4-5 ft. tall plants.

'Herbstschnee' is a compact cultivar with pure white petals and yellow centers. Plants reach about 3 ft. in height.

'Purple Dome' is a true dwarf variety of New England Aster. Bright purple flowers cover wide-spreading, 2 ft. tall clumps throughout late summer and early fall.

Compact 'Herbstschnee'

With a Goldenrod cultivar

WHERE TO PLANT

Wherever they are planted, New England Asters fill out the garden in fall with lavish color. They look good in large perennial borders, near water features, and in wild meadow gardens.

Mass New England Asters as a backdrop for shorter plants in a perennial border, or place groups of them among shrubs, where their flowers in shades of pink and purple will create a dazzling display together with the bright fall foliage.

As New England Asters grow well in damp soil, they are an excellent choice to plant along streams or near ponds. They even do well in boggy, low-lying areas and will spread quickly.

Tall New England Asters bring structure and stunning color to meadows and wild gardens, where they can spread, seed themselves naturally, and mix together with wildflowers.

Pink and purple Asters are stu

PERFECT PARTNERS

The beautiful, clear-colored flowers of New England Asters glow in the cool light of autumn, enhancing many other perennials and shrubs that bloom in fall.

Plant several 3 1/2 ft., white-flowered 'Autumn Snow' New England Asters around a clump of 5 ft., pink-flowered Boltonia 'Pink Beauty' for a soft, airy effect.

For a brighter effect, place deep lilac-flowered 'Treasurer' New England Asters behind a group of 'Margarete' Japanese Anemones, with dark pink, semi-double flowers.

'Alma Potschke' is one of the most brilliantly colored

...ning in this perennial border

New England Asters. Its red
buds, opening to deep pink
flowers, are wonderful
combined with ornamental
grasses such as Maiden Grass
or mixed with Sunflowers for
a last burst of fall color.

...ibrant 'Alma Potschke'

PLANTING & AFTERCARE

YOU WILL NEED: ❑ Established New England
Aster plants ❑ Spade or shovel ❑ Compost ❑ Rake

1 Divide New England
Asters every few years,
when clump is overcrowded.
In early spring, dig up entire
clump with a shovel.

2 Rinse excess soil off
roots. Pull or cut clump
into pieces, each with 3-5
shoots and vigorous roots.
Discard woody center.

3 Before replanting,
prepare soil. Spread an
inch or two of compost over
area and work it into soil.
Rake planting area smooth.

4 Dig a hole for each
division, spacing them
18 in. apart. Set divisions in
holes, spreading out roots.
Firm soil around plants.

5 Water plants well. As
divisions have usually
suffered some root loss, be
sure to water frequently until
they are well established.

Tip

To keep New England
Asters more compact and
promote larger flowers,
pinch off the tops of the
stems in late spring.

Secrets of Success

BUYING HINTS

- **Buy** New England Asters in gallon containers in spring or fall. Choose young plants with healthy foliage.
- **Avoid** overgrown or rootbound plants as they will not transplant well. Do not buy plants with signs of powdery mildew.

SUN & SOIL

- **Full sun** to partial shade. New England Asters grow best in full sun. In hot climates their flowers last longer in partial shade.
- **Average soil.** New England Asters can tolerate poorly drained soils that remain wet in winter.

SPECIAL ADVICE

- **Even after** being pinched back, tall varieties may need staking. In early summer, place bamboo stakes around clump and tie with twine.
- **Do not give** New England Asters fertilizers high in nitrogen, which can lead to rank, leggy growth.

 ## Seasonal Tips

LATE WINTER
Starting seeds
Sow Aster seeds 8-10 weeks before the last frost date. For best germination, sow the seeds in six-packs, place in plastic bags, and set them in the refrigerator for two weeks. Set six-packs in a warm, bright area for germination. Harden off before planting outdoors.

SUMMER
Watering
New England Asters grow naturally in fairly damp areas and need watering during summer dry spells. Avoid getting water on leaves.

FALL
Deadheading
To prevent too many volunteer seedlings, remove faded flowers before the seeds mature *(below)*.

 ## Plant Doctor

Asters are susceptible to powdery mildew, evidenced by a white film that covers leaves and stems, eventually causing them to die. To avoid infection, keep plants well watered and grow in an open area where air can circulate. Cut out and dispose of infected parts.

Oriental Poppies

Exotic flowers in luminous, fiery colors

Season	Special Features	Best Conditions	
P Perennial	✓ Easy to grow	🌐 Zones 3-8	
✱ Flowers late spring to early summer	✂ Good for cutting	Full sun	
		Well-drained soil	

Flamboyant Flowers

The exotic blooms and colors of the Oriental Poppy are flights of fancy for the garden.

COLORS & VARIETIES

Oriental Poppies must grow for two years before they bloom, but the striking, fiery flowers are well worth the wait. The 6 in. wide, goblet-shaped blooms offer shades of red, mahogany, orange, white, and salmon. The petals, grouped around a simple seedpod, resemble colorful sheaths of crepe paper, with deep purple or maroon at their bases.

The bristly, coarse, green leaves of the Oriental Poppy

The brilliant central seedpod

'Henfield Brilliant' in a bed

reach 10-12 in. in length. The foliage dies back in mid-summer, often reappearing in early fall and persisting throughout the winter.

Oriental Poppies have deep taproots that do not like to be disturbed and do not transplant well, so decide on a good, permanent location before you plant.

For luminous colors, choose the watermelon pink 'Glowing Rose', or the bright white 'Pinnacle'. Unique colors include the brilliant, orange-scarlet 'Harvest Moon' and the stunning, silver-edged, deep salmon blooms of 'Victoria Dreyfus'.

WHERE TO PLANT

Oriental Poppies prefer a sunny location with very well-drained soil. They are best in flower beds that need a dose of explosive color.

Add drama to a perennial flower garden by including a swathe of spectacular Oriental Poppies. Their showy, silky blooms are sure to take center stage among other perennial flowers.

Cut-flower gardens are not complete without Oriental Poppies. Grow the pure ivory 'Barr's White', and the crinkled, white and deep pink blooms of 'Show Girl' for a dazzling display.

In a foundation planting, Oriental Poppies offer a bonfire of color for a sun-drenched, lightly colored wall of your house.

Oriental Poppies planted throu

Along a path, facing west toward the sunset, the bright Poppy blooms look as though they are on fire.

PERFECT PARTNERS

Oriental Poppies are sure to steal the show from their companions, so plant them with flowers in subtle, cool shades or with those that continue their color when the Poppies' hues fade.

Interplant the luminous apricot 'China Boy' with gold or orange Marigolds and Dahlias that will fill out as summer progresses.

Silver foliage plants, such as Russian Sage or 'Silver King' Artemesia, are stunning with Poppies. Set

ghout a perennial flower bed

off these smoky grays with the carmine 'Big Jim'.

White flowers are perfect complements to the stronger Poppy hues. Mix 'Beauty of Livermore' with Nicotiana's fragrant, ivory blooms.

The fiery 'Allegro Viva'

PLANTING & AFTERCARE

YOU WILL NEED: ❏ Bareroot Oriental Poppies ❏ Builder's sand or compost ❏ Shovel ❏ Upstart

1 **Prepare the bed** several weeks before planting. Sprinkle 4-6 in. of builder's sand (compost in clay soil) on soil and dig in 12 in. deep.

2 **Mix the Upstart** with water according to package directions. Soak the Poppy roots in the solution for several hours.

3 **Plant so that** the tops of roots are 3-4 in. below the soil level. Allow 18-24 in. between Poppy plants. Plant in groups of three.

4 **Mulch with compost** for winter protection. Label the Poppies' location so you know where they are when spring arrives.

5 **In spring,** sprinkle some compost around the Oriental Poppies. Feed them with an all-purpose granular fertilizer for best blooms.

Tip

For enduring floral displays, cut Poppies early in the morning, sear cut ends in a flame, and place them in water.

Secrets of Success

BUYING HINTS

- **Buy bareroot** Oriental Poppies through catalogs in summer for a fall planting. Alternatively, look for root cuttings at a nursery.
- **Avoid container** plants in fall, as Poppies confined to a pot all summer may not survive transplanting.

SUN & SOIL

- **Full sun.** Although they grow poorly in hot, humid conditions, Oriental Poppies prefer a full day of sun where summers are cool.
- **Well-drained soil.** Good soil drainage is crucial, as exposure to standing water can rot the roots.

SPECIAL ADVICE

- **Large-flowered** Oriental Poppies may need staking, and all should be protected from wind to prevent stalks from breaking.
- **The seedpods of the** Oriental Poppy make lovely and unusual additions to dried-flower arrangements.

 ## Seasonal Tips

EARLY SPRING
Planting
If you live in zones 3-6, you can plant bareroot Oriental Poppies now. Fertilize older Oriental Poppies with an all-purpose 5-10-5 fertilizer.

LATE SUMMER
Mulching
Provide your Oriental Poppy plants with a layer of well-rotted manure or compost as a mulch.

FALL
Planting
This is the best time to plant

Oriental Poppies in the garden. Plant bareroot Poppy plants as soon as possible once you have purchased them. Plant healthy, 6 in. root cuttings horizontally, 2 in. deep in the soil.

 ## Plant Doctor

Blackened flowers and leaves with water-soaked spots are signs of bacterial blight. Dig up and destroy infected plants. Do not plant Poppies in that location for two years. Allow the soil to dry completely before planting other flowers.

Penstemons

Showy, tubular flowers in rich, vivid colors

Season	Special Features	Best Conditions	
Perennial or annual	Good for cutting	Zones 3-11	
Flowers in summer	Attracts wildlife	Full sun	
	Drought resistant	Well-drained soil	

A Favorite of Hummingbirds

Blooming profusely along tall stems,
Penstemons are vibrant additions to the garden.

COLORS & VARIETIES

Also known as Beard
Tongue, Penstemons
produce many tubular
flowers in bright reds and
blues, as well as purple,
pink, salmon, white, or
bicolors. The 18-36 in. stems
have oblong, green leaves
along them and at their base.

Of the many Penstemon
species, Foxglove Penstemon
(*Penstemon digitalis*) is one
of the hardiest, surviving to
zone 3. It has lovely, ¾ in.
long, pure white flowers on
18 in. stems.

Many beautiful hybrid
Border Penstemons, often
grouped as *P. x gloxinoides*,
are perennial only in mild
areas (zones 9-11);
elsewhere, they are grown
as annuals. These include
named varieties, such as the
3 ft. tall, bright red 'Firebird'
and mixed-color strains like
'Sensation Mixed', all with
extra-large flowers, over 2 in.
long and wide.

Bright 'True Blue'

In a vibrant bed along a patio

WHERE TO PLANT

With their preference for
warm locations, Penstemons
fit in well in sunny borders
and rock gardens.

Sharkshead Penstemon
(*P. barbatus*) is especially
well suited to a hot, dry
garden, where its long,
loose, 3 ft. tall spikes of
bright red flowers glow in
the heat of the summer sun.

Somewhat more
compact forms of the
Sharkshead Penstemon, such
as the 2 ft. 'Rose Elf' with its
masses of deep rose blooms,
are excellent choices for
large rock gardens and
butterfly gardens.

All of the hybrid
Penstemons are delightful
additions to the middle of a
perennial border. Group
three or more 'Holly's White'
or deep purple 'Midnight' for
an effective display.

'Evelyn' surrounded by Cynoglo

PERFECT PARTNERS

The many colors and bicolors
of Penstemon flowers lend
their blooms to intriguing
partnerships in the garden.

'Husker Red' Penstemon
is a form of Foxglove
Penstemon, with bronze-
purple foliage topped by
glistening, white blossoms. It
provides a long season of
interest when combined with
a purple-leaved Barberry and
edged with Cottage Pinks or
silvery Lamb's-ears.

Plant deep red 'Garnet'
Penstemon as part of a hot-
colored border with other
vivid red and yellow
bloomers, such as Red-hot
Pokers, Scarlet Sages, Yellow
Cosmos, and Daylilies.

ssum 'Firmament'

Choose Penstemon 'Huntington Pink', which has lovely pink blossoms with contrasting white throats, to complement a pastel pink-flowered Shrub Rose, such as 'Kathleen Ferrier'.

Vibrant 'Rainbow Mix'

YOU WILL NEED: ❏ Penstemon plants ❏ Shovel or spading fork ❏ Compost ❏ Fine gravel

1 Improve drainage by digging in a 2-3 in. layer of compost. Dig a hole for each plant the depth of the container and 4 in. wider.

2 If soil is heavy clay, mix 1 in. of gravel into the bottom of each hole to improve drainage and prevent crown rot.

3 Set each plant in its hole, spreading out the roots. The crown of the plant should be slightly higher than the surrounding soil.

4 Firm soil around the roots and water well. Use fine gravel for mulch, rather than organic matter, to discourage crown rot.

Dollar Sense

Penstemons last only a few years, but new plants are easy to start from cuttings. Cut 3-4 in. long stems just below a leaf set. Remove lower leaves, dip ends in rooting hormone, and insert 1 in. apart in damp perlite. Cover with a plastic bag. Transplant cuttings when rooted.

Secrets of Success

BUYING HINTS

- **Buy potted Penstemons** with healthy, green leaves in spring in cold winter areas. In warmer climates, buy plants in fall.
- **Avoid plants** with drooping foliage or any signs of rot, indicating they have been overwatered.

SUN & SOIL

- **Full sun.** In most climates, Penstemons are happiest in full sun. In very hot regions, they prefer some afternoon shade.
- **Well-drained soil.** While Penstemons can adapt to soils low in nutrients, good drainage is essential.

SPECIAL ADVICE

- **To save Penstemon** seeds, empty open seed capsules into an envelope and keep in a cool place for six weeks before sowing.
- **Give perennial plants** little or no fertilizer, as rich soil causes them to fill out nicely, but die quickly.

Seasonal Tips

LATE WINTER
Sowing seeds
Start seeds about eight weeks before your last frost, pressing them gently into the surface of sterile potting mix. Keep in a cool location, at about 60 degrees F. Seedlings should begin to emerge in 10-15 days.

SPRING
Setting out seedlings
Harden off Penstemon seedlings before setting in the garden. Do this by placing them outdoors in a sheltered spot for a few hours each day. Plant in the garden after the last frost.

SUMMER
Cutting back
Cut back stalks after the first blooms (*below*). This encourages plants to bloom again later in summer on side branches.

Plant Doctor

Penstemons may be bothered by the Fuller Rose beetle. Actually a weevil, the $1/3$ in., black-brown pest eats plant leaves at night. Collect beetles in the morning by laying a sheet under the plant and shaking it. Gather up sheet and put in a pail of hot soapy water.

Peonies

A spectacular, carefree spring delight

Season	Special Features	Best Conditions	
P Perennial	**⚬** Some varieties: fragrant	**⊕** Zones 4-8	
✸ Flowers in spring	**✓** Easy to grow	**☀** Full sun	Height: 2-4 ft.
	✂ Good for cutting	**⚘** Well-drained soil	Spread: 2-4 ft.

Extravagant Blooms

Peonies are a springtime favorite for their exquisite forms and fragrant blooms.

COLORS & VARIETIES

Peonies are valued for their easy care, long life, and unparalleled, multipetaled flowers. The plant's lush, compact, deeply cut, green foliage provides a striking background for summer bloomers and often a hint of autumn color.

Peony flower forms range from singles and semi-doubles to full doubles in hues of white, red, purple, and every possible shade of pink. The double 'Festiva Maxima' is a pearly white favorite flecked with tiny dots of crimson.

Many of the single, Anemone-like blooms, like the white 'Ivory Jewel', have bright yellow centers. The single blooms of 'Scarlet O'Hara', however, are a solid, spirited, fiery red.

WHERE TO PLANT

Peonies grow in open mounds or clumps and develop into a stunning

P. mascula along a fence

display planted singly, in rows, or in a mixed border.

For a riot of spring color, create a border hedge of Peonies along a fence or driveway. Edge a brick patio to accent the plants' rich green foliage and to enjoy their sweet scent, which is reminiscent of old Roses.

Fit this long-lived plant into a large shrub border where it will bloom for years.

Plant Peonies in a winding perennial bed where the attractive foliage anchors summer bloomers even after spring blossoms have faded.

Adorn an entry area with the enchanting fragrance of classic, soft pink 'Sarah Bernhardt' or the elegant, wine red hue of the popular 'Port Royale'.

PERFECT PARTNERS

The broad range of flower colors and delicate, deeply cut leaves of the Peony complement a wide range of

'Festiva Maxima' paired with L

flower and foliage forms, shrubs, and grasses.

Nestle the violet-blue, saucer-like flowers of Cranesbill or the dainty, pink blooms of Coral Bells in front of clumps of the sturdy 'Cornelia Shayor' Peonies. The blooms on this double-flowered variety are rose-pink upon opening, but gradually fade to blush white.

For a dazzling display, combine the tall, graceful spires of a deep purple Siberian Iris with the enchanting, double, early, pink-blooming 'First Lady'. Later, add bright annuals, such as Transvaal Daisies, Vinca, or even Impatiens for a constant display of color throughout the summer.

The frilly 'Gay Paree'

ily 'Amaretto'

Under a hedge of the rich green summer foliage of 'Gold Standard', plant low-growing, silver-green foliage plants, such as Artemisia 'Silver Mound' or Lamb's-ears 'Silver Carpet'.

The showy Japanese Peony

PLANTING & AFTERCARE

YOU WILL NEED: ❏ Bareroot Peony ❏ Spade ❏ Compost ❏ Granular fertilizer ❏ Mulch

1 In fall, dig a hole at least 18 in. wide and deep. Enrich soil by mixing with compost. In highly acidic soil, add 1 cup of lime.

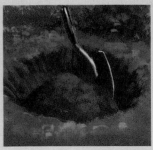

2 Mix granular fertilizer or a handful of bone meal into bottom of planting hole. Replace soil mixture to form a cone inside.

3 Place roots over cone so that the top roots are no more than 1 in. below surface. In colder regions, position buds 1 ½ in. deep.

4 Gently cover Peony roots with soil. In colder regions, add a protective layer of organic mulch after ground is frozen.

5 In the spring, work mulch amended with fertilizer or compost into surrounding soil, away from emerging shoots.

Tip

Peonies require winter chilling. In warm areas, select adaptable varieties or periodically apply ice to the dormant roots.

Secrets of Success

BUYING HINTS

- **Buy bareroot plant** divisions in fall with healthy root systems and at least two healthy buds.
- **Avoid plants** with soft or dry, shriveled roots, or small root systems. Do not buy Peonies without identifying labels.

SUN & SOIL

- **Full sun.** In hot areas, light shade in afternoon is best, especially for pastel shades, which have a tendency to fade in hot sun.
- **Well-drained soil.** Peonies tolerate a wide range of conditions, but prefer slightly alkaline soil.

SPECIAL ADVICE

- **Although manure is** a useful fertilizer, it should be avoided with Peonies. Its nitrogen content can burn and rot sensitive roots.
- **Peonies perform** best with no competition from trees or lawn. Keep a 12 in. mulched area around bushes.

 ## Seasonal Tips

FALL
Planting & Dividing
Plant out new Peonies. Dig up mature (10-year-old) clumps, lifting entire root mass. Use a sharp knife to separate Peony roots into sections with at least three to five eyes. Replant.

EARLY SPRING
Maintaining
Carefully move winter mulch away from emerging Peony shoots and work it into the surrounding soil. Add a balanced fertilizer or a layer of compost to plants.

LATE SPRING
Staking
Tall Peonies with large flower heads may require staking. Use either metal hoops (*below*) or individual stakes for support. Remove side shoots to get larger flowers.

 ## Plant Doctor

Excessively wet spring or winter conditions can cause botrytis blight, turning Peony buds black and wilting foliage. Remove and destroy affected plant stems and provide ample air circulation. Some fungicides are also effective.

Pinks

Old-fashioned, fragrant, cottage-garden flowers

Season	*Special Features*	*Best Conditions*	
Perennial	Good for cutting	Zones 4-9	
Flowers in late spring or summer	Evergreen	Full sun	
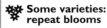 Some varieties: repeat blooms	Fragrant	Well-drained soil	Height: 6-18 in.
	Good groundcover		← Spread: 9-18 in.

Geraniums

PLANTING & AFTERCARE

YOU WILL NEED: ❏ Pinks in 4 in. containers ❏ Compost ❏ Spading fork ❏ Trowel

1 To improve drainage and add nutrients in planting area, spread a 3 in. layer of well-rotted compost. Dig into top 8 in. of soil.

2 Dig holes the depth of containers and several inches wider. Space small varieties of Pinks 6-8 in. apart, larger ones 12-18 in.

3 Remove plants from containers and loosen tangled roots. Place in holes so they sit at same depth as in containers. Water well.

4 As Pinks age, the centers of the plants may die. Sift a mixture of sand and compost into bare area to spur new growth.

double, white flowers on strong stems, in a cottage garden border with blue Bearded Irises 'Marhaba' and Delphiniums 'Blue Nile', sparked with magenta-flowered Rose Campions *(Lychnis coronaria)*.

Edge a flower border with drifts of 'Musgrave's Pink', white-flowered Cottage Pinks with unique green eyes, or pale lavender 'London Delight', alternating with low drifts of silver-leaved Lamb's-ears.

Dwarf Cheddar Pinks have many wonderful rock garden partners. Combine the small, double, ruby red flowers of 'Tiny Rubies' with dwarf Candytuft 'Little Gem' and violet-blue Dalmation Bellflowers or Campanulas 'G.F. Wilson'.

Dollar Sense

To replace declining Pinks, take heel cuttings—a side shoot pulled off with a piece of stem—in summer. Place in pot of damp perlite. Cover with plastic bag and keep in bright spot out of full sun. Transplant to 4 in. pots. Set in garden in fall in mild-winter climates. Wait until spring in colder areas.

Bright Buttons of Color

Pinks feature fancy-fringed, lacy blossoms over tidy mats of silvery foliage.

COLORS & VARIETIES

Pinks form low clumps of narrow, silvery blue leaves that send up slender, 6-18 in. stems topped with spicily fragrant, single to double, 1-2 in. wide flowers. Not all Pinks have pink flowers— some bloom in white, rose, red, or salmon, many with contrasting centers.

Old-fashioned Cottage or Grass Pinks *(Dianthus plumarius)* bloom in summer. These cottage garden classics bloom in the full range of Pink colors, with 'Dad's Favorite' bearing double white flowers.

Modern hybrid Pinks include 'Doris', with pale pink, semi-double blooms. They flower repeatedly from late spring through summer.

Maiden Pinks *(D. deltoides)* spread into loose mats of 6 in. tall foliage, with charming, ¾ in. flowers hovering above in early summer. Both bright scarlet 'Zing' and rose-red 'Zing Rose' are popular varieties.

'Flashing Lights' among rocks

Brilliant 'Crimson Treasure'

Cheddar Pinks *(D. gratianopolitanus)* make neat mounds of foliage, covered in summer with dozens of flowers on 6-10 in. stems. 'Little Joe' has crimson flowers, while 'Spotty' has dark pink flowers flecked with white.

WHERE TO PLANT

Plant Pinks in open, sunny places in the garden where their spicy fragrance and charming flowers can be appreciated close up.

Cottage Pinks are an excellent choice for edging a Rose garden or Peony bed, especially along a brick path where the Pinks can spread to soften hard lines.

Plant mat-forming Maiden Pinks, such as 'Microchip', a mix of red-, white-, and pink-flowering plants, on a bank as a showy, blooming groundcover.

Compact Cheddar Pinks are a delightful addition to patio containers. They are also lovely when grouped

'Ideal Violet' in front of Hardy

A pink edging of 'Little Jock'

around taller plants in a raised bed near an entryway.

PERFECT PARTNERS

The colorful blossoms and clean foliage of all Pinks make them ideal companions for many other border or rock garden plants.

Plant long-blooming 'Haytor' Pinks, which have

Secrets of Success

BUYING HINTS

- **Buy Pinks in 4 in. pots** in early spring. Purchase seeds or plants with healthy foliage and a few buds to show the flower color.
- **Avoid Pinks** with limp, wilted foliage. Do not buy plants with dark spots on their leaves or stems.

SUN & SOIL

- **Full sun.** In most climates, Pinks bloom best in full sun, but appreciate a little afternoon shade in very hot areas.
- **Well-drained soil.** Good drainage is important, especially in winter when plants are not growing.

SPECIAL ADVICE

- **Rabbits may eat** foliage of Pinks in winter. Protect the plants with chicken wire or Pine boughs.
- **The 'Alpinus' variety** of Pinks is especially hardy; it will survive zone 3 winters. These Pinks are easily raised from seeds.

 Seasonal Tips

EARLY SPRING
Starting seeds
Sow seeds, purchased or collected from garden plants, in containers indoors four to six weeks before last frost. Or, sow directly in garden after danger of frost has passed. Pull back winter mulch on existing plants.

SUMMER
Shearing
Shear off faded blooms *(right)* with hedge clippers; apply fertilizer, and water. Many varieties will rebloom in a few weeks.

LATE FALL
Covering
In zone 6 and colder, cover plants during winter to protect them from cold. Use a light mulch of evergreen boughs, wood chips, or shredded leaves.

 *Plant Doctor*

Alternaria leaf spot is a fungal disease that appears as dark purple spots with yellowish brown margins on the leaves and stems of Pinks. Badly infected plants often wilt and die. To prevent the spread of this disease, destroy infected Pinks plants and avoid wetting the foliage.

Purple Coneflowers

Rugged natives with pincushion centers

Season	Special Features	Best Conditions	
P Perennial	✂ **Good for cutting**	🌐 **Zones 4-9**	
❋ **Flowers in summer**	🐦 **Attracts wildlife**	☀ **Full sun**	Height: 3-5 ft.
	✓ **Easy to grow**	⛏ **Well-drained soil**	◀—Spread: 1-1 ½ ft.⌐

A Sun-loving Wildflower

Purple Coneflowers provide a long season of beautiful blossoms in hot, sunny areas.

COLORS & VARIETIES

The 4-5 in. wide, Daisy-like flowers of Purple Coneflowers *(Echinacea purpurea)* feature dark, beehive-shaped centers and grow on strong, 3-4 ft. stems over rough, lance-like, dark green leaves.

The wild or species form of Purple Coneflower has drooping, pink-purple petals. Varieties are available that also offer shades of white and red, such as 'The King' with deep carmine flowers and creamy 'White Lustre'.

'Bravado' has extra-wide, lavender-pink petals that are held flat around the central cone, rather than drooping like other Coneflowers.

The rose-pink petals of a close relative, Tall Coneflower *(E. pallida)*, droop gracefully on tall, 4-5 ft. stems.

A natural butterfly attractant

WHERE TO PLANT

Purple Coneflowers are at home in formal perennial borders and wildflower gardens alike. They are also an excellent addition to a cut-flower garden.

With their long season of bloom, pretty Purple Coneflowers are the mainstay of summer borders. Include several varieties in a bed of sun-loving perennials.

The deep crimson-pink flowers of 'Robert Bloom' Purple Coneflowers glow against the dark green background of a hedge or in front of a gray stone wall.

Create a colorful garden specially designed to attract butterflies by combining Purple Coneflowers with Butterfly Weed, Jupiter's Beard, and shrubs such as Butterfly Bush and Spiraea.

PERFECT PARTNERS

With their wonderfully clear flower colors and tall stems,

Purple Coneflowers in a prair

Purple Coneflowers blend well with many other plants.

For a bright, effective combination that blooms for weeks, combine rosy pink 'Bright Star' Coneflowers with white and blue varieties of Mealy-cup Sage and the yellow Daylily 'Hyperion'.

In a large border, intermingle drifts of 'White Swan' and dark carmine

'Bravado' and Black-eyed Susa

The unique 'White Swan'

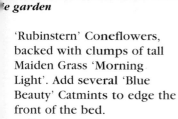

e garden

'Rubinstern' Coneflowers, backed with clumps of tall Maiden Grass 'Morning Light'. Add several 'Blue Beauty' Catmints to edge the front of the bed.

In a sunny prairie garden, combine rose-red 'Magnus' Coneflowers with golden Coreopsis 'Zagreb', tall Goldenrods, and 4 ft. native Switchgrass.

ns

PLANTING & AFTERCARE

YOU WILL NEED: ❑ Purple Coneflower plants ❑ Shovel ❑ Compost for clay soil

1 **After the last frost,** dig a hole 1 ft. deep and several inches wider than the container for each plant. Space 12-18 in. apart.

2 **If the soil is** heavy clay, mix a shovelful of compost into soil in the bottom of each hole. Remove plant from container.

3 **Set the plant** in its hole, adding more soil, if necessary, so that the plant will be at the same depth it was in the container.

4 **Fill in around** plant with soil, firming it around roots with your hands. Water to settle soil and eliminate air pockets.

5 **As plants bloom,** deadhead to encourage more flowers. For volunteer plants, leave some flowers to mature near the season's end.

Dollar Sense

In spring, check for volunteer seedlings. Dig up when they are 3-4 in. tall and immediately transplant to a new area.

Secrets of Success

BUYING HINTS

- **Buy Purple Coneflower** plants in gallon containers in spring. As the plants will not yet be in bloom, look for a label naming flower color and variety.
- **Avoid plants** that are overgrown or have limp or dried-out leaves.

SUN & SOIL

- **Full sun.** Purple Coneflowers bloom best if they receive direct sun for at least six hours each day.
- **Ordinary, well-drained** soil. The roots may rot in heavy, clay soils. Add compost or sharp sand to improve drainage.

SPECIAL ADVICE

- **If you collect** seeds from your plants, sow ¼ in. deep in flats and leave out over winter. Water in spring.
- **If purchased seeds** germinate poorly, try pre-chilling. Mix seeds with moist sand and refrigerate for four to six weeks.

 ## Seasonal Tips

 ## Plant Doctor

LATE WINTER
Starting seeds
Start seeds indoors eight to ten weeks before your last frost date. Keep seedlings in a cool, brightly lit location *(below right)*. Transplant into garden when 4 in. tall.

FALL
Dividing
When clumps become crowded, usually after four years, dig them up and rinse off the soil. Cut or gently tease apart roots into sections and replant.

SUMMER
Maintaining
Though Purple Coneflowers tolerate dry soil, they will bloom best if watered weekly. In rich soils, the stems may become top heavy when in bloom and will require staking.

Purple Coneflowers, generally pest-free, are susceptible to attack by Japanese beetles. The ½ in., shiny, green adult beetles chew flowers and leaf tissue between the veins. To control, knock beetles from plants into a jar of soapy water and let sit overnight.

Shasta Daisies

Classic summer flowers for brilliant elegance

Season	Special Features	Best Conditions	

Perennial
  Blooms from summer into fall
	✔ **Easy to grow**
	  Excellent cut flowers
		Zones 4-8
		 ▦ **Full sun or light shade**
		 ⬟ **Moist, well-drained soil**
			
			 Height: 2-4 ft.
			 ← Spread: 2-3 ft.

Wondrous Wildflowers

A single Shasta Daisy plant will produce a mass of simple and charming blossoms.

COLORS & VARIETIES

Shasta Daisies are members of the same family as garden Chrysanthemums. They bear blooms up to 5 in. wide, featuring white or yellow-hued petals set around a gold, button-like center. The long-lasting blooms make excellent candidates for cut-flower arrangements.

Some newer Shasta Daisy varieties are double-flowering, holding twice the number of petals of a normal flower. Dwarf forms are also available. 'Esther Read' is a double-flowering variety that grows 18 in. tall.

WHERE TO PLANT

Shasta Daisies are great for filling in gaps in a perennial border, or creating a meadow garden design. They can also fill bright, full-sun beds with masses of flowers.

The snowy white flowers will vibrate against the deep

Rudbeckia and Shasta Daisies

green hues of an evergreen hedge or a brightly colored fence. Be sure to plant the Shasta Daisies along the sunny side of a barrier.

Accent the length of a garden path with the casual, country look of these plants.

Choose compact Shasta Daisy varieties for planting in large, rustic containers, such as half-whiskey barrels or cedar planters.

Combine these versatile plants in a bed of wildflowers with similar flower heads in summer shades for an elegant meadow design.

PERFECT PARTNERS

The simple, white blooms of Shasta Daisies make ideal companions for flowers in any color of the rainbow.

Tall, spiky flowers, such as Foxgloves, Delphiniums, and Gladioli, offer sharp contrasts in form to the

Shasta Daisies in a mixed bed

Shasta Daisies shine against p

circular flowers and mounded shape of the Shasta Daisy. Fuse these towering flowers, in shades of violet and blue, with the cream hues of 'Cobham Gold'.

For vibrant color and a country ambiance, combine the 6 in. wide blooms of 'Majestic' with the bright, summer hues of Purple Coneflowers, Clara Curtis Daisies, Golden Marguerites, and Black-eyed Susans.

Lower-growing annuals, such as Petunias, Geraniums, and Marigolds, can be used at the base of the Shasta Daisy to fill in around the

Purple Irises and red Peonies

bare stems. Combine these annuals, in shades of pink, red, and orange, in a container with the compact form of 'Little Miss Muffet'.

A mass of 'Little Miss Muffet'

PLANTING & AFTERCARE

YOU WILL NEED: ❏ Potted Shasta Daisy ❏ Shovel ❏ Compost ❏ Mulch ❏ Bone meal

1 Dig a hole that is 1 ft. deep. Add a shovelful of compost to hole and mix well. Carefully remove the Shasta Daisy from its pot.

2 Set the plant into the hole, adding more soil if necessary to bring plant to a slightly higher depth than it was planted at before.

3 Fill in around the plant with more compost mixed with soil so that the area is slightly mounded. Water thoroughly.

4 Mulch around the Shasta Daisy to keep its roots cool and moist, but avoid getting mulch in the center or crown of plant.

5 Feed Shasta Daisies with a natural organic fertilizer, such as bone meal, just before (and two weeks after) they bloom.

Tip

Taller Shasta Daisies may need staking to keep the heavy flowers from toppling over in summer storms.

Shasta Daisies

Secrets of Success

BUYING HINTS

- **Buy Shasta Daisy** plants anytime during the growing season. Choose plants in single pots that are lush, green, stiff, and upright.
- **Avoid Shasta Daisies** with soft, mushy centers or those that have black spots on their foliage.

SUN & SOIL

- **Full sun or light shade.** A half-day of sun is essential for Shasta Daisies to bloom. Direct sunlight will produce the largest flowers.
- **Well-drained soil.** Shasta Daisies will bloom in average soil, but add some compost for better blooms.

SPECIAL ADVICE

- **To keep tall** Shasta Daisy plants compact, pinch flower stalks after they start to grow. You will get more, but smaller, flowers.
- **Divide clumps** of Shasta Daisy plants every second year to grow them as vigorous perennials.

 ## Seasonal Tips

FALL
Planting
Plant container-grown Shasta Daisies and remove flowers after they have bloomed.

EARLY SPRING
Dividing
Lift and split apart older plants. Replant divisions from outside of the clump and throw away the older middle section.

LATE SPRING
Pinching
For more compact plants, remove the top 2-3 in. of

growth from each stem *(below)*. Stake plants now before they grow too tall.

SUMMER
Maintaining
Keep soil moist, but not wet. Cut for indoor use and deadhead spent blossoms.

 ## Plant Doctor

Lace bugs are insects with lacy wings that cause deformed Daisy leaves and blooms. First signs include gold-green spots on tops of leaves and brown droppings on bottoms of leaves. For severe infestations, spray with insecticidal soap.

Perennials for Sun

"Flowers have an expression of countenance as much as men or animals. Some seem to smile, some have a sad expression, some are pensive and diffident, others again are plain, honest and upright."

—*Henry Ward Beecher*

INVITE BUTTERFLIES into your perennial garden by planting splashes of red, purple, pink, and gold sun-splashed blooms. Butterflies are attracted to the vibrant hues of Delphiniums, Penstemons, Purple Coneflowers, Gloriosa Daisies, and New England Asters. Other magnets for these fluttering creatures include such perennials as Butterfly Weed, Queen Anne's Lace, Rockcress, and Joe-Pye Weed.

INSTEAD OF STARTING SEEDS IN BIG flats, consider using space-saving containers such as plastic baked goods cartons or salad-bar containers. Plastic cartons with clear, hinge-top lids make wonderful mini-greenhouses. The lids let in light and retain moisture, providing the humidity that seeds need in order to germinate.

RECYCLE OLD OR TORN LAMPSHADES for use in your garden. Save money buying hoops at garden centers by supporting Peonies, Delphiniums, and other top-heavy perennials with the metal frames of lampshades.

HERE'S A QUICK WAY TO DETERMINE whether or not your seeds will germinate: Place a few seeds from the packet on a hotplate. If the seeds jump off the hotplate, the rest are worth sowing. If the seeds remain on the hotplate, chances are that the others from the same packet will not sprout.

GIVE PERENNIALS THE NUTRIENTS they need, and recycle water at the same time. Don't throw out the water you used to boil eggs; let it cool, and then sprinkle over plants. Do the same when you need to empty your fish aquarium: Pour the nutrient-rich water over your plants instead of down the drain.

Nature's Way

Self-seeding plants—such as Coreopsis, Gloriosa Daisies, Heleniums, Lavateras, and Lupines—sometimes change with each generation if they come from different parents. You may be pleasantly surprised by the results of your volunteer seedlings, which may include exciting variations in flower colors and forms.

December
- Water perennial beds well before severe weather, since frozen soil will not allow water to get to plants.
- Mulch perennials when ground freezes to prevent frost from heaving up your plants.
- Send for seed catalogs.

January
- Begin ordering perennial seeds from catalogs.
- In areas with mild winters, begin digging over beds.
- This is a great time to sketch out plans for a new perennial garden or to redesign the layout of an existing one.

February
- This is the month to start sowing perennial seeds indoors for summer beds.

March
- Protect spring-flowering perennials from slugs and snails by encircling plants with a ring of ashes or crushed eggshells.
- Dig and fertilize beds that will be planted soon.
- Remove weeds as they sprout up.

April
- Begin hardening off the perennial seedlings that you started indoors.
- Start planting summer-blooming perennials in garden; amend soil with plenty of compost.

May
- Take cuttings from spring-flowering perennials to get more new plants for free.
- Stake or provide support for tall flowering stalks in windy sites.
- Continue weeding beds.

June
- Cut back or deadhead spent flowers; let some go to seed.
- Check perennials for signs of pest and disease damage.
- Make sure plants are watered regularly.

July
- Collect seeds from spent flower heads and save for future sowing.
- Continue watering beds and add fertilizer.

August
- Sow seeds outside now for next year's blooms.
- Pick flowers for drying indoors, so that you can enjoy summer perennials in dried bouquets in fall.

September
- Since the weather is unpredictable in cooler regions, prepare for sudden temperature drops by placing young seedlings and tender plants inside a cold frame.
- Divide overgrown perennials that have finished blooming.

October
- Purchase spun-bonded row cover, which will keep light frost off of perennial plants but will still let air, light, and water in.
- Rake leaves out of beds.

November
- Mulch perennial beds to protect plants from harsh winter temperatures.
- Cut back perennials.

Winter

Spring

Summer

Fall

INDEX

INDEX

INDEX

INDEX